SWALLOWING CLOUDS

Swallowing Clouds

An Anthology of Chinese-Canadian Poetry

Edited by
ANDY QUAN &
JIM WONG-CHU

ARSENAL PULP PRESS
Vancouver

ARSENAL PULP PRESS
103-1014 Homer Street
Vancouver, BC Canada v6b 2w9
www.arsenalpulp.com

 The publisher gratefully acknowledges the support of the Canada Council for the Arts and the B.C. Arts Council for its publishing program.

Canadä The publisher gratefully acknowledges the support of the Government of Canada through the Book Publishing Industry Development Program for its publishing activities.

Typeset by the Vancouver Desktop Publishing Centre
Printed and bound in Canada

CANADIAN CATALOGUING IN PUBLICATION DATA

Main entry under title:
Swallowing clouds

ISBN 1-55152-073-7

Canadian poetry (English)—Chinese-Canadian authors.* 2.
Canadian poetry (English)—20th century.* 1. Quan, Andy. 1.
Wong Chu, Jim, 1949-
ps8283.c5s92 1999   c811'.5408'08951   c99-911012-8
PR9195.35.C54S92 1999

Contents

INTRODUCTION 7

PAUL YEE 11

RITA WONG 21

LOUISE BAK 33

GOH POH SENG 49

MARISA ANLIN ALPS 61

SEAN GUNN 73

JAMILA ISMAIL 81

LYDIA KWA 87

FIONA TINWEI LAM 97

EVELYN LAU 109

KAM SEIN YEE 121

LARISSA LAI 133

LAIWAN 145

LEUNG PING-KWAN 153

LIEN CHAO 169

GAIK CHENG KHOO 179

THUONG VUONG-RIDDICK 187

GLENN DEER 199

ANDY QUAN 205

RITZ CHOW 219

PEI HSIEN LIM 231

JEN LAM 235

FRED WAH 253

PAUL CHING LEE 265

JIM WONG-CHU 273

ACKNOWLEDGEMENTS 286

PUBLISHING CREDITS 287

PHOTO CREDITS 288

Introduction

This anthology of poetry comes from a place that is both real and mythical—a place that exists concretely, and one that is created as we speak its name: *Chinese-Canada*. What does it mean? Is it a legacy from the seventies, from the polysyllabic policy of multiculturalism? Is it a population explosion from the seeds sown in Chinese diners across the country? Urban Chinatowns that sell snow-bound Canadian cities in plastic domes imported from Asia? Is it growing up eating dinner with chopsticks and watching American sitcoms every afternoon?

I would guess that every writer *and* reader of this collection will have their own idea of what it means. Me, I admit to ethnocentrism. For years, I thought of Chinese-Canada as *my* Chinese-Canada, North American-born descendants of the villagers of Canton who arrived in Canada to build the railroad, or search for gold, or escape the famine of the early 1900s, all in search of a better life.

But as I grew older and looked at the Chinese-Canadian "community" around me, I had to see how diverse a people we were. Not only from Canton, immigrants came from all parts of China, from Taiwan, and from bustling Hong Kong. Perhaps they arrived in Canada by way of other continents, via Europe, Africa, Latin America, and Australia, or East Asian countries such as Malaysia, Singapore, Indonesia, and Vietnam. The poets of *Swallowing Clouds* are these travellers, and their children, and their grandchildren, and even further down the family tree.

It is a diverse group such as this that can give meaning to a name. *Chinese-Canada*. And if the poets here are all to be grouped together in a Chinese-Canadian poetry anthology, then we are witnessing multiple creations. First of all, it is the creation of a community, a "we" rather than "I", a gathering of diverse people who presume a cultural coherence due to our "Chinese"-ness. Next, we see how this characteristic of race and culture attaches itself to a nation-state, the great snowy vast plains and water country—oh, Canada. And then we see what creativity, what creations in the form of poems come out of this place, location, community, and culture.

So how does one start to talk about these creations? To begin with, the writers themselves: such diversity that it is probably easier to talk about the differences between us than the similarities. The poets in this collection include activists, full-time writers, academics, students, an editor, a doctor, a postal worker, and health-care workers. A few are known internationally, some have published many books, others are launching their first, and still others are publishing in magazines and journals, or reading their works aloud on stage. We have come to our poetry along different pathways as well. Some of the writers included here are better known for novels, short fiction or children's books than poetry. Some poets first published amidst an Asian activist movement in the 1970s. Others have built their reputation outside Canada and are now becoming better known here. A significant number have published their work through feminist journals and gay and lesbian publications.

What do we have in common? Poetry, first of all. All of us have come to express ourselves in an art form that receives relatively little attention in contemporary Canada, and has a bad reputation as being either inaccessible because people can't understand it, or too accessible because people can't avoid running into someone who admits they write poetry. So, we're joined together in being outcasts. Poets? *Bah.*

But outcast is a good word to describe us in more than one way. I've heard a story that long ago people made no separation between poetry and sacred truth. Today, in some Eastern European countries, poets are still regarded as national heroes, keepers of history, voices that speak for a people, that can bring down governments. I think it is fair to say that while poets are not otherworldly, we're at least a little unusual.

We're also outcasts in terms of our position in society, no matter which specific location that is. The term "ethnic" or "visible minority" of my youth has turned into "people of colour," but it means the same thing to us whether born in Canada or not. The colour of our skin, our race, makes us different. Differences in language—language being a window into different ways of seeing—as well as the experience of immigration lead many of us to ask the question: "Where do we belong?" Some of what empowers the work in this anthology is the alien glance: someone from the outside looking in and seeing something that hasn't been noticed before.

We're not just looking in, though; we're tapping on the glass. We're walking through the door and bringing in the outcast, taking the outsider inside. Art can be an egotistical act; as it is created partly to say "I am here," it inevitably draws attention to its creator. With our poems, we're also saying a bit of that. *We are here.* But I think that the tone of voice will be a mixture of confidence and self-consciousness, part questioning and part assertive. For in being part of an anthology such as this, we are identifying ourselves as "minority" writers at the same time as we are entering and altering and creating a "mainstream."

Looking back, it has taken us to this very moment to produce the first anthology of Chinese-Canadian poetry. While early Chinese immigrants scratched poems into the walls of the detention cells of West Coast immigration centres, and wrote of their loneliness in poems mailed back home in the early 1900s, these works were hidden from view from the rest of the nation. The first works of poems and short fiction by Chinese-Canadians would start to appear in literary journals and magazines only after a Canadian literary scene burst forth in the 1970s.

In 1979, *Inalienable Rice*, a Chinese- and Japanese-Canadian anthology, was published by the Powell Street Revue and the Chinese Canadian Writers Workshop, two grassroots arts organizations based in Vancouver. It included articles, fiction, poetry, and photographs, the first collection of its type. In 1981, the magazine *West Coast Review* published a special edition dedicated to Asian Canadians and the Arts. In 1991, *Many-Mouthed Birds,* the first anthology of Chinese-Canadian short fiction and poetry, appeared. Since its publication, writers such as Denise Chong, SKY Lee, Larissa Lai, Evelyn Lau, and Wayson Choy have gone on to publish nationally and internationally acclaimed books, and Paul Yee and Fred Wah have won Governor General's Awards.

Now, the Canadian literary scene is bursting with fresh talent and voices from a variety of multicultural backgrounds. Many magazines and journals have produced special issues featuring writers of colour. The Chinese-Canadian Writers Workshop has become the Asian-Canadian Writers Workshop and publishes a regular magazine, hosts workshops and events, and sponsors a contest for new Asian-Canadian writers. What better time to publish the first poetry anthology from Chinese-Canada.

A final explanation and a final musing: the title of the anthology *Swallowing Clouds* could hint at any number of images: a ravenous giant devouring the heavens? Perhaps a goddess flying through cloud banks while wisps of white flow delicately past her lips? A celestial banquet with nine courses that disappear into vapour as soon as you begin? In fact, the phrase refers to the ubiquitous Chinese specialty, *won-ton,* the Cantonese pronunciation of two Chinese characters together equalling cloud and swallow: the heavens a clear, salty broth and the clouds beckoning you to take them into your open mouth. It's daily life made both poetic and mythical by the Chinese; metaphors contained in the most humble dumpling.

I was told in my travels by friends from China that it is best never to say that something is good. *Mama huhu* is a better phrase for someone of Chinese origins to say, they explained. Two horses, two tigers, meaning, "not bad." I took this as a lesson in Chinese modesty and caution and wondered if two horses and two tigers were "not good" because they were neither one thing nor the other. I admit that I didn't learn this lesson well, for I'd like to praise the poets in this anthology in immodest terms. In embracing multiple identities, exploring diverse themes, and expressing bicultural and multicultural realities, there is a particular spark and life to this writing. I hope that you devour it with pleasure.

—Andy Quan
Co-editor
June 1999

Paul Yee

PAUL YEE is a third-generation Chinese-Canadian who was born in Spalding, Saskatchewan in 1956. He grew up in Vancouver's Chinatown, where he had a "typical Chinese-Canadian childhood, caught between two worlds, and yearning to move away from the neighbourhood." He attended the University of British Columbia and has written and published widely. His books include the non-fiction works *Struggle And Hope: The Story Of Chinese Canadians* and *Saltwater City: An Illustrated History Of The Chinese In Vancouver;* and the following books for children and young adults: *The Boy in the Attic, Breakaway, Roses Sing on New Snow, Tales from Gold Mountain, Curses of Third Uncle, Teach Me to Fly, Skyfighter,* and *Ghost Train,* for which he won the Governor General's Award in 1996. He currently works as an archivist in Toronto.

Kamloops Chinese Cemetery (July 1977)

The grass was a heavy blanket
lifted
and there is sand
sifting down the slope.

Here and there
a brick
a block
of raw stone
squared by uneven hands
but set with care
to mark the mounds.

Here and there
uprooted and thrown
lengths of wood
cracking, breaking, flaking
bearing your names.

These were your markers.

Once, people knew you
and brushed your name
with velvet ink
and carved your village
       your death
       your year
onto these wooden planks.

Wood, because
no one
wanted to stay,
but carved
because they could not forget.

Operation

They've opened a hole in my side
and reached in
with sterile hands
tearing out
painlessly,
a part of me
my name, my history
that never existed.
Not that I cared.
They tore out the roots of my black hair
one by one,
that they would grow again
a different colour.
They cut out my eyes
dropping in blue marbles to take their place.
I was blind, even before.
And since I was short
like most Chinese
they stretched my spine,
slowly,
joint by joint
crack by crack.
Then it hurt
and I screamed.

Hastings Express, 10 pm

At the Chinatown stop
the bus is invaded
seven chattering women
loud in Toisanese
laughing and leering.

I shut my eyes
and feign a sleep.

Later
one eye peeks open
there's a white lady
across from me
legs clenched in silence
under a leather armour.
Small eyes glare
like cheap earrings.

If she feels threatened
I'd join her army.
I was a deserter
from long before.

Spences Bridge, B.C.

These desert hills
baked in time
have locked him away.

His shadow alone
would cool
this desperation.

A fence
rusted wire and ragged timbers
vanishing proof
straggles over sheeted slopes.

Nothing is left.

Only a rasping wind
grates the squinting earth.

Sagebrush under dry pines
Rubble rolling downhill
Sandy browns, grey and green.

Rock to rubble
Dust to ringed sun
Mountains are moved
and railways are laid.

Last Words II

Forget us
if you must.

But if you must
remember us,

We were young men

Broad of shoulder
and supple as bamboo.
We lived early mornings
Stretched and rippled
in the hazy fields
laid tracks to the horizon.
At break of work
We cooked rice
and ate as brothers.
There were our women,
they waited at home.
We waited,
but only the bosses came
the canneries came
the mines died
and cooks started up.

We could send
letters home.

The Grass Dragon

For Jim Wong-Chu, who had the idea, and the Chinese
Cultural Centre, who had the festival

Pender Street is silent this Sunday morning.
Early cooks pass by
rub sleep from their eyes
and wonder who we are.
And we are gathered
with our cleavers and our clippers.
The kung-fu kids can't stay still
and slash with them, and play kill.
The rest would rather sleep awhile.

The farm is forty minutes away
the grass is long and moist
just what the master ordered.

Grass for our grass dragon
yet to be awakened
grass from the Fraser soils
weave body to legend.

We unload ourselves from the truck
and survey the field
but how do you start? We're city people
suddenly free.
We've never seen the earth
from our knees.

We spread out to work,
hand-clench the grass, pull it taut,
cut it away, near the root,
lay it aside,
and move on.

The grass grows wild and sharp
we dig for gloves.
Our knees are wet and black
and we squat, instead.

There's a jug of tea, Chinese pastries,
two loaves of uncut bread, and cheese,
green plums from the deserted orchard.
We're hungry and we come together
but there are parallel parties of echo:
Chinese bounces by us
and they can't catch our laughs.
Still, we're smiling at each other.

We are back in the earth
bent and pulling, cutting and aching
thankful for the merciful clouds
and pray that the rain will wait.
(Was it like this in the rice paddies?)

The grass we tie into bundles
piled high in the driveway.
At two we make a chain
pass our labour onto the truck
linking a bed that we jump into
for a sweet trip home
together.

We come again, three times more
we sail out earlier
sweep further up the valley
for the finest
long grass, lean and supple.
Dragon grass, seeded from hope and daring.
And this dream ripens into gold
as our harvests rise higher
sweating in a Strathcona garage.

And the festival drifts close
as the autumn moon swells full.

We are underground carpenters
scattered throughout Chinatown.
In the warehouse basement
long handfuls of grass are coiled
wrapped into tendons for a rippling whip
now at ease, laid door to door, back and forth,
waiting for the thunder of heavy drums
and the running, rolling feet
to pump life and fire and fury
through its straw dry veins.

In another basement
up Pender Street
more hands cast a noble head
raising a wooden snout high
like a prow flanked by proud eyes
and soaring whiskers of curled foil.

It will be the first:
girls have never run the dragon poles.
We have never seen this dragon
or known its tradition.
Joss sticks to fan out from its life core of grass,
stabbing the moon with a million bristling glowing eyes
It will catch the screams of the children
pound Pender Street in a new beat
spark memories of old China
exploding in a new cloud of firecracker incense
and summon us, to celebrate
our first dragon
made in Canada.
We can only wait.
We can hardly wait.

Rita Wong

RITA WONG grew up in Calgary and currently lives in Vancouver. She has taught English in China, Japan, and Canada, and has worked as a writer, an archivist, and an activist. Her work appears in the anthologies *The Other Woman: Women of Colour in Contemporary Canadian Literature, Another Way to Dance, Millennium Messages, Hot and Bothered,* and *Kitchen Talk.* Wong received the 1997 Asian Canadian Writers' Workshop Emerging Writer Award. Her first book of poetry, *monkeypuzzle*, was published by Press Gang Publishers in 1998.

chaos feary

upon reading vandana shiva's biopiracy

pyre in pirate bio in bile
mono in poly breeder in
womb pull of landrace allo
me poietic auto me diverse
trans over genic harassment
over seas genetic as pathetic
as engine of disease socio
me catastrophe political and
eugenic organ as an ism
general as the mono startle
of a soma ethic under
trodden patent as in lies
hubris as in corporate
culture as in american
military as a choking tentacle
as pollution erodes these lines
no sense in food or rhyme
resistant as in herbicide or
people lost and found field a
factory dinner a roulette
conquest as in seeds hands as
in fist

grammar poem

write around the absence, she said, show
its existence
demonstrate   *this is*
its contours   *the sound of*
how it   *my chinese tongue*
tastes   *whispering:* nei tou
where   gnaw ma? *no*
its edges   *tones can*
fall   *survive this*
hard   *alphabet*
on my stuttering tongue, how its tones &
          pictograms get flattened out by the
                  steamroller of the english language,
live   its etymology of
half-submerged   assimilation
in the salty home of   tramples budding
my mother tongue,   memory into sawdusty
shallows   stereotypes, regimented capitals,
              arrogant nouns & more nouns,
          punctuated by subservient descriptors.
      grammar is the dust on the streets waiting to be washed off
by immigrant cleaners or blown into your eyes by the wind. grammar
is the invisible net in the air, holding your words in place. grammar,
like wealth, belongs in the hands of the people who produce it.

denim blues

there are denim mountains in my closet:
well-worn cutoffs, raggedy jeans,
adolescent skin-tight pants, baggy prairie overalls,
years of tacky stampede outfits

nothing comes between me &
the labour of the garment workers
their fifty cents a day sweat
hugs me tight every morning

my auntie's fingers nimble
with the demands of piecework
how she churns dozens of jeans by dim lamplight
one more casualty for casual wear

cotton picked by hungry workers
beaten into fabric & submission in far-off factories
dissembled into department store offerings

black denim with amputated
fingers waving bloody threads from pockets
knotting in my chest as i look in the closet
find nothing to wear

nothing, that is, but
thin faded gauze ripping open,
spilling labour into consumer vision,
ragged with guilt, ignorance, fear
but still rippling, a necessary banner
in the wind for change

reading my dinner

i listen to the city hum
its endless murmur of buses,
exploitation, crime, industry

as i eat
proteins gurgle
corporate betrayals
slide their way to
my stomach acids

difficult to nourish justice
on the supermarket shelves
every choice
a link in the faulty chain

a songbird warbles of food
on southern tables
the demilitarization of stock markets.
RRSP this!

there is every reason not to laugh
the newspaper a litany of reasons
not to laugh.
only intuition at the back
of my throat says
a loose hand is faster
than a tight one
only laughing & crying
can i survive the violence
of everyday transactions

lips shape yangtze, chang jiang, river longing

three gorges, you whisper
the sound of rocks filling your mouth:
we, who have always been displaced by poverty,
sent across the ocean to find rice

i look for the big sky   but clouds suffocate me
rain defeat for the dispossessed.
families pushed out of homes, mouths gaping hunger.
stone soup, stone face,
cracking as earth reveals herself through us

throat. gorges. the glottal stop rising into my nose
pressure on my lungs one hair away from unbearable
the heaviness: signing the dotted line
when you cannot read what you've signed

without memory, we die fast & brutal
flooded by greed
our drowned, bloated arms wave
and who will wave back?

the sound of rock breath
falls empty onto diasporic spray
light wet on black hair

we miss the boat, even as we disembark

sunset grocery

the summer i am afraid of fire i make change in my sleep. the cash register's metallic rhythm comes quick to my fingers: 59¢ from $1 gets you back one penny, one nickel, one dime, one quarter. can do this backward & forward quick as the machine's kachink, but i prefer stocking shelves. prefer to avoid customers making snotty sing-song accents, avoid men flipping through porn. open nine to nine seven days a week, the store is where i develop the expected math skills: $60 net one day divided by twelve hours is $5 an hour, divided by two people is $2.50 an hour, or divided by five people $1 an hour.

groceries have the corner on small details. i count the 20,000 times i breathe each day. sell cigarettes i am not allowed to smoke: player's light, export a, du maurier. nicotine variations, drum & old port. popsicles, twinkies, two percent milk. faced with 7-up, coffee crisp, bottles of coke, i retreat into hundreds of books. by grade four i learn the word "inscrutable," & practice being so behind the cash register. however, i soon realize that i am read as inscrutable by many customers with absolutely no effort on my part, so i don't bother trying any more. ten years of this means you can one day leave when someone takes your place. what changes?

a skinny hallway connects three bedrooms in the back. in the room we share, my sister talks in her sleep. our dog Smoky often snores by the bunk bed. down the hall my father snores too. some nights, it's hard to tell who is louder—the dog or my dad. the nights are noisy with all the things never said in the day.

the summer that i am afraid of fire, i hold Smoky every
night until the fear subsides. until my heart slows enough
that i can sleep. her stinky breath comforts me, reminds
me of the many senses we have to discover fire before it
finds us. that summer, i always have a glass of water near
my bed. not enough to put out flames, i can at least drink
when i awaken, throat dry, sweaty & fearful in the night.

maybe because i am a fire girl, sparked between my
parents' loins in more romantic times, i know the power
of fire, how it warms me in cold prairie winters, how it
simmers, boils & stirfries countless meals in the steaming
kitchen, how it rests hungry within me, waiting for the
tinder of another body. maybe the fear stems from fire's
power to destroy, to erase an existence eked out from
penny nickel dime tedium. to consume in minutes what
took years to build.

one ear always attuned to the bell of the opening door i
find i can't trust or tell a straight story. what if flamboyant
prometheus had been an archer shooting down suns
instead of bearing fire into human hands? i draw witches
with pointy hats & greenblack hair, dragon ladies in salem
garb, learn of ancient chinese secrets from american
laundry soap commercials. between amazons, milwaukee
factory girls, flying nuns, customers come in, customers go
out. rabbits, cheese, women populate the moon. flame
throwers light the sky with their arms' circular logic.

part fire, part water, part air & part earth, i try to distance
myself from the fire within, fear that i cannot control its
random blasts. i learn to cultivate that part of me which is
earth, sowing gradual seeds of pragmatism, small quiet
sprouts in the spring, studious endeavours reaping
scholarly harvests, parental approval, respectable tunnels
for escape.

as months grow into years, the fears go undercover, as do
the dreams. the connection between night & day is too
painful & so each morning i cross the river of waking
washed clean of nocturnal memory. the price for a
respectable daytime existence is high. it is my own desire.
creating a vacuum, the hollow space which i become.

when i return to the grocery store years later, that long
echoing childhood hallway seems dark, crowded, needing
new carpet, clean linoleum, anything to open it up, clear it
of so many night words still unheard.

puzzlinen

blood red dye #3
iron chink fish gutter
tins   rust

put into knit penguin purl two & woven baskets
strandmade   berry-dyed in woof cones weft china
thread proceeds to east timorese rebels
chinese students grassroots africville   doing
language slow consciousness juggle   fishgasp & leap
struggle with what   put your toe on   slide –
grasp for rail   de-railed   juggle jaguar grin bear
children & stories   maybe this that ribbon other or sprigs
on crazyquilt patch   sprigs on underwear before rip

fury channel
push

to oceans jump   to mountains track   over over over
not yet   to photographs tell   to trunk open over
only   laundromats always open   sundays even
punch the cash register over   cheap food
pull the door   it won't open   for you
what's wrong   you
everyone else   can
they don't see it   laugh
basket   chase
re   run
suzy wongs   pocahontas! run!
give them   hot food?
rotsa raffs   voice? what voice?
you must   make this up

parchment

this globe my body so dry its surface flakes white, the only time this skin is white. upon contact, your eyes on my skin write an old tale, words we know too well. with time, we wrestle new stories from each other, nets rip with each sweaty assertion. we are not all the same. the trail of saliva leads here to your tribe & my tribe in this room private as the histories in our stretched muscles. i mark you with my fingers, my hair, my teeth. inscribe my body's anecdotes upon you so that you cannot name me foreign. i speak myself against you, year after year, replenish the oasis in this desert. you will learn my dialect as i have learned yours, the pages of our exchange rustling a new tribe. a pact, you & i, a pact.

down south peachwomen:
minimum wage pickers

	calloused the gingerknobby
	hands perform
broken willow baskets	the tongue stinging persimmon
plum kids out	of sore cherry wombs
squish	pomegranate seeds tart drops of
memory	traintrack over bigfooted bodies
	chew chew chew that fruit
	you wish but your job is to
	pick the merchandise

can we catch a rhythm catch a train   c'mon can we
escape the pesticide curse
get paid what we are worth
pidgin women unite

unite who? wudja mean by workers?
:listen: peachpickers hummm
one she picks, another she cans, another cooks
it means rhubarb pie & more
       feasty days of noodles & rice & fish & tofu &
       pork & dumplings & chicken & bean soup;
sung in the kitchen. sung into existence, ya'd think.
sung & sweated & worried & wrung. dishcloth hung.
flat as a green onion pancake & even greasier.

you can do it: factory   kitchen   fields.

Louise Bak

LOUISE BAK works actively as a writer, editor, radio broadcaster, performance artist and sexuality counsellor. Her writing has appeared in numerous magazines, journals, and anthologies. Her first book of poetry, *emeighty*, was published in a limited edition by Letters Bookshop in 1995; this was followed by *Gingko Kitchen* (Coach House Books, 1997). Along with being the current guest art editor of the feminist culture magazine, *PlusZero,* she serves on the board of directors of the magazine *Fireweed*. Aside from her literary (in)ventures, Louise can also be heard every morning as co-host of *Sex City*, Toronto's only morning program dedicated to ongoing cultural (s)excavation (CIUT-FM 89.5). Her performance work has appeared in many venues and independent films, including *Cheese* (1995), *Amidst Us* (Total Eclipse Productions, 1996) and *Brothers and Sisters* (1998). She is one of the co-producers of *SLANT*, Canada's first video magazine to explore Canadian-Asian art and culture, now in development. She recently completed her M.A. on women's involvement in Cantonese opera in Canada at the University of Toronto . Some of these poems will be in her forthcoming book from Coach House.

Listening

Silent and lotus-postured under the maple tree,
thinking of Buddha's bodhi sprouting in my body.
3 branches dip down like the 3-legged triskelion,
rising and setting to the rhythm of the Serpent
that slides between the descant of the whales,
the timpani of the gorillas and the low whispers
of human voices, ingrained in every truncheoned
annular time ring and pericoloured torn-leaf tangram.

Mongolian *khummii* meditators call to me from the
cardboard box, thrown into the crusher by 2 garbage
collectors across the street. Watching the grumbling
truck's jowls close on another ubiquitous piece of
Chinatown's Great Wall of refuse, rebuilt everyday
by grocers, peel-spitters, and the solitary women who
mutter about the neodesic properties of marriages
that rely on temerity and laconic root-lies to survive.

I overhear a bruised neighbour call it *wan*-redress,
while another names it *manji*-pleonasm, desire, that is,
inescapable as they slowly circle half-bled *lik-kiep*
of relocated narcosis and promise. Sweeping back
and forth before me. I try a little to put the confusing
sounds together. Just then, a woman pushing a baby
stops beside me, telling me how strange it is to move
so far to Canada and still end up in the *Namib* desert.

My hypochondria(xles) roll panicked at the feelings
of isolation in a folded city, growing tauter with each
anaesthetic moan. I remember ah-poh telling me not
to mistake resuscitative breathing with just CPR, like
the time she was scared when a giant grouper swam up
beside her. Its pectoral fins were the same size as her
flippers, and its dark body was heavily scarred like the

atrophied 3-inch lotus hooks she listened for as a child.
I see her again weaving through a loud mass of Chinese
bicyclists, who assertively thumb tinny handbar bells,
alternately touching or knocking down strangers with
shoulder-pole loads. She stops and takes my hand
as I move from the tree, making the noise of the grouper
opening its mouth, exposing rows of gill rakers. Cleaner
fish and wrasses, listen intently for such a yawn, from
inside the carnivore's mouth, heard as a signal to enter.

Triskelion: symbolizes perpetual rising and zenith setting. Linked to the mythical
serpent, it denotes Gnostic wisdom and strength.

Khummii (or diphonic method): involves a sustained note sung in tandem with
certain mouth cavity movements that created a droning harmonics, quite unlike
anything heard around the world.

The Chinese call the swastika a *wan*, while the Japanese call the swastika a *manji*.
The swastika is one of the oldest symbols in the world, with the earliest Sanskrit
word itself meaning "well-being." The attempted co-optation of this sign by the
Nazi Party and its usage in contemporary Neo-Nazi organizations have
transformed the meaning of this symbol to reflect racist and hateful references.

Lik-kiep: refers to the myth of the holy menstrual calendar plant in Chinese
tradition, on which an observed pod grew every day for 14 days, then a pod fell off
every day for 14 days. When the lunar months became jostled by solar reckoning,
the Chinese added extra days when a pod withered without falling off.

Namib: a desert; "an area where there is nothing" in the Nama language of Namibia.

Ah-poh: grandmother (Cantonese).

Double-Take

yellow earth scorched red

red sorghum rusted with blood

blood of thin white hare shot

shot by sake-gunners retching

retching over bleeding flesh

flesh of young slave girl's

     friend

friend who gnawed her pants

pants ravished with toothmarks

toothmarks like her own on

on soldier's bootless foot kicks

kicks her on to wooden board

board called plank of comfort

     woman

woman as cum-vessel for rice

rice extra-salted with tears

tears after those double "U"s

"U"sually "U"niformed maraud

maraud her mother and sister

sister watches firefly's light

eclipsed

eclipsed by a cloud of grenades

grenades air-popping a kernel

kernel of life they called whore

whore-before-woman beside hare

hare only knew till now that this

this was a **woman**-*before-whore*

whored by war.

Twin-Squatting

it was always cold in the unheated theatre;
a porn film house on weekends. the girls
stood about in yellow blancmange leotards.
of course they were not dancers at all, but
scabrous reminders of a childhood, unfaded
when they made a sister disappear in fear

their mother who could barely distinguish
between them, told them both twice that
a poor woman's cumwork is never done,
before she demanded they both become
women early in the money bower, where
they say the devil never wears out his cock.

       Hematuria started to give up smoking
       at twelve, by limiting the matches, swallowed
       while she stared out of the flubbing window.
       she hardly noticed the rhythmic trundling
       of her body under another body, she wished
       was like the cylinder of wire-netting they put
       up to protect a young tree, before they felt
       the dull ticking of the adding machine
       calling them again. she stared back at
       the stars like so many goo-goo eyes, peeping
       from the dripcastle sky, where the paper goddess
       was always crying like micro-popping corn.
       her gown edges were all puckered and ashen,
       with a paper crane upended in the folds.
       she noticed its tail was burned while a bright fire
       still flamed from its wet choice-tremoring belly.

Anhedonia saw a swing when she turned fourteen,
eighty-eight seconds before her sister. she didn't
share how its top was flush with the clouds,
and the suspension ropes attached to it were
dangled loose; nobody was playing on it, so
she approached it. she swung forward to the
rude volley of calf-eyed children. she swung
backward to the flaps of their overbright jowls.
her life resembled a speeding tube train
with the driver slumped heavily over the lever,
flashing by station after station of unbuckling cravens.
it stopped when it reached the guide-line goddess
in the *plaza de toros*. she tried to show her how
to grip a bull's horns and swing up and over each time,
propelled by the animal's head jerk. suddenly,
the sacral console appeared not unlike their mother.

she entered the house to find her pale sister
in pyjamas of parachute silk, soaked in a pool
of blood. over-lip ripped, her mouth looked
like a punctured petunia or the doddery hearts
of Eng and Chang, feigning specimen status
while scorned for being born too close.

listening to the chink-chink-chink of a chisel on
the gravestone, her goddess vanished behind a
backdrop of stitched cloudbanks. gone, right after
she ran away from their suburbiton home in the cover
of a city arborescing and nesting their twinned face
with the rumbirds, singing in twos at each antedawn . . .

Hematuria: bloody urine.

Anhedonia: a condition in which pleasure or orgasm in sexual behaviour is lost;
thought to be the result of certain head injuries.

M.

M. Chrysanthemum
M. Butterfly
M. Saigon

What next?

M. Bangkok?
M. Malay?
M. *Chin*-a (Pet)?

all silently chanting
Colonize Me
a mantra for the White-myth-maestro

dreaming of *wai tu yung* girls
dispensing rices cakes on open clam shells in a parade

pondering whether her waiting cunt
is slanted to match her eyes

imagining lotus blossoms teaching you
Hau tu Sekkusu

hoping her soul is as yielding as silk
not stone-washed like *Levi's* denim

Occidentally constructing the myth of
Asian woman as exoticized cipher

en garde:

M. Commodifier
M. Pearl Fisher
M. Colonizer

your chrysalis is rupturing
and the butterfly is flying free
no longer your frenulum flutterer.

Hau tu Sekkusu: "how to sex" (Japanese).

Mina Tulpa

she unlocks the cell and allows the prisoner
to get ready for her discharge
   instead of the usual asterisk smile of joy
   she beckons her inside for a lengthy talk
   about doing time
      undoing them both like the quiet mina
      who could be heard loudly last night
      over furious coughing and screaming fits
         repeatedly woke her from the warden desk
         never spotting any movement
         from face-down position under the covers
         she snored an unwaking dent into the pillow
         on every flashlight inspection
            convinced the noises were caused
            by atmospheric pressure distorting
            the ticking of the bedside clock
               she did not expect to find her sister shivering
               and collapsing into a chair
               refusing to be released in the morning to go home
                  to their home near an aerodrome
                  where she claims she stood in the basement
                  flooding as she saw a Disney animatronic figure
                  who looked like the Little Mermaid
                  caught between a stationary wall and a moving wall

she listens noticing the whites of her eyes
turning greenish and her head suddenly
growing broader like a blinking lantern atop a pole
   receding into the chair she speaks of light
   rejoining a smashed body
   cell by cell in the form of their mother
   encased in the pillow last night
      dressed in glittering layers of metal foil

that once covered hot in-flight meals
her head was bleeding in the cockpit
with fingers that moved like a cannula
under her skin to spell remembrance
drained post-flight while the mina managed
to squeeze its way through the prison bars
   and they both simultaneously remember
   how she still flew while lying in the hospital
   with a complex tangle of tubes
   like the sewer rat's bevelled teeth
   entering and exiting her body
      doctors extracted a roll of bills inside her vagina
      hiding twenties to ritually resist the spectre
      of urban poverty and liver cirrhosis
      circling their oblating home
        returning to the natal heartwood
        she stares at the grain in the door
        twisting the key in mimicry of her sister
           with proud purpose but reluctant to enter
another haunted timetable prison
where she recalls the robber who looked like father
stealing mother's wedding ring
just after she was newly widowed
and ululating for him in her sleep
   entering she scraps her last reserve of crack
   in favour of the clear haze
   she sees surrounding an old photo of mother
   in a Douglas C-47 spraying thousands
   of gallons of insecticide at treetop level
   spelling mass mosquito death
      while the mina tulpa always survived
      travelling over a shifting trapezoid of faint lights
      outlining a liquid hole in a tarn of imagineer sleep
        radioing that she was coming back
        losing altitude fast
        she crashed it into the elusive glow
        of release like a dorado

setting a goodbye on the water-clock alarm
with the plane-tail section waving always
out of the TV at them in the 6 o'clock news
never new.

Mina: talking bird of starling family (Hindi).

Tulpa: Buddhist mysticism's notion of a magical entity created by concentrated thought, which may have a will of its own.

Cannula: thin metal wand used in liposuction, which is plied back and forth under the skin.

Dorado: blue and silver sea-fish, which displays brilliant colours when it dies out of water.

Shame Shadow

for Ruan Lingyu (1910-1935)

in this world of many people
i think my heart is made
from hexagonal islands of glass
with no two heartbeats ever the same
    they are all irregular
    when all my dreams are seeing her
                body quiver
                with a frisson of happiness
                    a sensation she'd never dreamed
                    could be hers in life
                    when she was alone
                    knowing that all kinds of people
                    could open the door and walk in
                        fact that was what the screen
                        was all about
                    a place to dismantle a life
                    so that all that remained
                    was a pile of fabric gestures
                    and a position to play voyeur to herself
before a three a.m. make-up call
as she watched peony snowflakes melting
on the poster of a fairytale temple
and some undecipherable English words
written on it
    thinking her life
    was somehow happy enough
    being called a *modeng nuxing*
            lucky to have moved to Shanghai in 1935
            a city they called the capital of the tycoon
                Paris of the East
                and whore of Asia
                    her name on a trod-upon newspaper
                    since that night when
                    they first held her hostage
                    to the whims of the press and money

for her persona time
filled with longing for the inkfish
and yellow croaker in the small fishing village
creatures she released from the hook
    which did not tell her
    what she would freely give
    would cost her at the end
            of the movie
            where they whisper

          shame

        shame on the electric shadows of women
        on the silver screen
        who hum in lost voices
        punctuating pleasure
        in the nebula of a ballroom
        out of the frame

    shame

        shame
        on the overhead shot
        where woman is seen
        as the centre of a blooming flower
    that can never finish her song
    about the wild goose
    that comes with letters in its claws

   shame

     shame
     on the woman who showed us
     how to love like the drone
     of a hive as it begins to swarm
     to the inner horizon
     where a part of her orb remains intact
     no matter how unclothed she is on sale

for hours i have stood outside
below Lan Caihe's moon
too afraid to ask you for a song
my ear was still sore from pressing hard
on history's suicide door
where the note you left is posted
              "gossip is a fearful thing"

        as it funnels us into the spectred mouth
        which spaces threated under the skin
        nasty body parts   handling parts
        my body this   my body that
        child whore   *bhat poh*

                    and it seems wrong to hear curses
                    for sensations i have never felt
            or misshadow the colour of my soul
            over the mirrored dissolves i express
                    along streets named after small madnesses
                    i am followed by the long hum
                    i heard as a little boy when every part
                    of my body was protected
                    through imaging a breath

            Keep away from her navel—it is the morning star
            Keep away from her teeth—they will bite you
        Keep away from her lotus mound—it opens a lifetime

now shame
            still tries to turn every face
        into laughing death masks
                    and imprint sadness
            on every nerve branch

that tries to trust
the collapse and valence
of love

love that sounds like
the willful quiet
forerunning a revelation

Ruan Lingyu: one of the greatest female stars in early Chinese cinema. She commited suicide at the age of twenty-five, because she could not bear the weight of the scandal, obsession, and shame associated with her lifestyle.

Modeng nuxing: a Chinese term frequently used in literature and film of the 1930s to refer to the "modern woman."

Lan Caihe: a female Taoist immortal who chants poetry to warn people of the fleeting aspects of life and its transitory pleasures.

Bhat poh: a colloquial Chinese term used to describe "uppity," "loose," or "shrewish" women.

Goh Poh Seng

GOH POH SENG
was born in Malaysia
in 1936. He
received his
medical degree from
University College,
Dublin, Eire, and
worked for twenty-five
years in Singapore. He
now lives in
Vancouver. He has
had three books of
poems published in
Singapore: *Eyewitness*
(1976), *Lines from Batu
Ferringhi* (1978), and
Bird with One Wing
(1982). A collection of his
selected poems, *The Girl from
Ermita and Selected Poems* was
brought out by Nightwood
Editions, in 1998. His first novel *If
We Dream Too Long* (1972) won the
National Book Development Council of
Singapore's Fiction Book Award and has
been translated into Russian and Tagalog. His
other novels are *The Immolation* (1977) and
Dance of Moths (1995). In 1983, Goh was
awarded the Singapore Cultural Medallion. His
works have been anthologized widely and have
appeared in numerous magazines.

Vietnam 1967

Beginning another vigil
he regards the tentative sun
through a fragmented sky;
otherwise there is only greenness.
In the still quiet dawn
he downs a mug of tea,
leans his rifle against a tree
and now and then recalls his home
unearths another day.
He is far from his hamlet.

It was an unquestioning life,
tilling the stubborn land that defies
the controlling hand of man.
There was consolation, now he knows
the laughter of his child,
the softness of his wife
who yielded to him at night.
So what if kingdoms topple?

His dream shakes the silent air.

He sees his home gutted in the sun,
he sees his wife, head blown off,
the body of his child strewn
among young stubble of padi.

For days he prowled that waste
unable to quell his hate.
How to mobilize that precise pain?

Time passes.
Now and then a recall of home:
she chants at night to their child
who smiles, remembering small mischiefs.
After losing them,
their absence remains.

He makes his fists into a power
fierce as one whose sinews
could manage the sun.

In the glare of the sun
the planes beautiful
like silver spears
come in an eddy of air.

Amongst battered tree trunks
his blood splatters
into uncanny flowers.

Over the gentle contour of hills
and the sea,
the happy young crew from afar
returns to the air.

Thinking of the Poet Tu Fu

Strolling out into the evening after work
before the dew settles on the grass,
the sky without a cloud is as wide
and is the colour of the sea;
so much so, the little dark boats in the distance
seem to be moving up to it;
I think of you, old grey-haired Tu Fu,
how this kind of setting
and this time of day
would move you to sing one of your poems.

Towards the west the same sun is setting
making dark the trees in my garden,
throwing large shadows on the grass
while Kasan, my young son
runs about, noisily playing
soldiers with his friend.
I wonder whether you'd approve
who have written so much against wars?

Alas, my friend, we too have our
endless wars, one thousand
two hundred and fifty odd years
after you have lamented,
"Wars still not ended" . . .
in Vietnam
the Middle East
now Czechoslovakia
and Biafra!
When Kasan is older, I shall tell him.

Now my good wife is cooking
our evening meal in the kitchen;
I wish we could have you to dinner
and though I have no jugs of millet wine,
I'd get a few beers from the fridge.

How we would talk and talk,
my friend.

In the fading light
little swallows are having their last fly;
a lone sea hawk surveys overhead
then dives for its prey . . .
my place at Lim Chu Kang
overlooks the Johore Straits.
The small *sampans* are returning,
each boat has a tiny, uncertain lamp.
Already the distant hills
are melting into the night.

Once the sun has dipped
it is so far away,
farther than the stars.
Our life has become a small matter
though our anxieties loom large.
Thinking of you,
it is so easy
to span the years.
These twelve centuries or more
have really wrought little change;
the condition of man remains
much the same, much the same.

My wife calls;
dinner is ready.
Dear girl, she has read
all my poetry and asked
when I would write
one for her.
She should know
she matters more to me
than all my poetry.
I think you would
understand that,
my old grey-haired Tu Fu.

Our Back Garden, Victoria Drive

So brief, really
are these weeks of summer
conjured out of our back garden,
that I should not hold on to them,
     simply let go.

     There,
     one sigh
     and they're gone
          forever

Gate of Heavenly Peace

We woke early that Sunday in the cabin,
watching the summer morning
wash up upon the lake shore,
the surrounding firs and junipers
on the sides of sprawling hills
flamed green in the fresh light,
the water calm, smooth as oil.

Suddenly, a flock of birds took flight,
scattering like pieces of white paper
blown across the clearing
filling the air with raucous cries.

Then our sons told us
about the massacre at Tian An Men.
They'd heard the news over the radio
around 3 a.m. Newfoundland time.
Ivy, our hostess, and wife of Calvin Payne,
had the radio on all night by her bedside,
either because she couldn't sleep
and needed distraction,
else wanted some reassuring tie
to the outside world,
here, in this secluded retreat
by the lake beyond Portland Creek.

"Some bad, bye!"
Calvin said, shaking his head.
"Two thousand people killed,
three times the population of Cowhead!"
That's the outport on the west coast
where Ivy and Calvin lived,
and where I was working as the local doctor.

"Shooting their own children!"
Ivy exclaimed, as she busied herself
preparing the traditional Jig's dinner
of salted beef and potato cake,
boiled turnips, carrots, and cabbage;
Calvin switched the radio to a favourite station
for their staple diet of Sunday morning country music;
we sat on the sunlit deck
listening to plangent songs
about unrequited love and broken hearts.

It was hard to focus on the fact
that they were mowed down
in the hundreds that day in China:
young men and women
chests and backs shot full of holes.

The night before, when the sky hatched stars,
Calvin and I sat out sipping Johnny Walker,
unlocking words in the darkness,
failing to sight the Northern Lights;
Calvin recounting the hard life
in these parts when he was a child,
before Confederation, Welfare, UIC,
before the much-loathed Resettlement,
before the road struck north.
And I was thinking,
after spending more than a year amongst these folk,
how hard life still is in this province,
with its underdevelopment, chronic high unemployment,
with the recent big cut in the cod quota,
the closure of fish plants on the coast.
The future's bleak for the children
who either depart to feed
factories and mines in Ontario,
else stay and eke out a living
jigging cod, snaring rabbit,

working the short lobster season,
repeating the harsh cycle of life
led by their fathers and forefathers.

My friend Calvin's an exception.
He has laboured hard since boyhood
and now owns Payne's Sales and Service,
operating a diesel and gasoline pump,
a Ford pick-up agency,
a Yamaha skidoo dealership,
the tender for snow plowing the roads in town;
in addition, he drives the school bus,
and only recently, won the concession
to clean up the Shallow Bay Provincial Park
on the outskirts of Cowhead.
Whew! He makes me breathless.
Ivy herself has charge of
the family grocery store
with occasional help
from her daughter-in-law, Kay.
Ivy, who was born and raised in rural Labrador,
says she's considered an outsider
in spite of having settled in Cowhead
for twenty years,
another reality about outports in Newfoundland.

As a doctor, I have often chided Calvin
for working too hard,
but he laughs and brushes me aside:
"I loves it, bye!
I'm fit and strong."
Perhaps he's haunted
by privations of his past.
Still and all, he retreats often
to this small cabin in the wilderness,
which he built with his boys some years before,
hauling in materials by skidoo and sled

in winter, the most accessible season;
rest of the year, the terrain's boggy and wet,
almost impassable.
Here, he can renew himself,
cast for sweet lake trout,
bag his moose for the year.
It's simply a good place to laze about,
a haven from the mad turmoil of the world.

Yet, from this same lake
just three weeks earlier,
they'd pull out the House girl
barely twelve years old,
too late for resuscitation
by the time they summoned me.
I remember her body
lying on the back of the battered Ford pick-up
vivid in a flowery costume,
her hair straggly and wet,
lips blue, cheeks like porcelain,
pupils fixed and dilated
like the eyes of the cod fish I've seen
flopped upon the decks of dories
when they come in with the catch
on late summer evenings
by the small town jetty.

At the House's home that afternoon
in Daniel's Harbour, an adjoining outport,
I saw the father, Big Max,
seated by the oilcloth-covered kitchen table,
beating his head hard with his large fists
and wailing for his darling girl:
"I can't live through this, Mother.
Don't ask me to live through this!"
I attended to the old grandmother
who'd passed out in her rocking chair

by the small front parlour,
rallied around by family and friends.
I kept hearing Max's implacable cry:
"I can't live through this, mother.
Don't ask me to live through this!"
All the while wondering why
he's addressing his crushed, weeping wife, Rosie,
rather than fate, or the gods.
Poor Big Max, he was wrong, of course.
He can live through this.

And so can we,
this infamous Sunday of June 4, 1989,
relaxing on this near-pristine lake,
watching the air dancing above the water,
the golden light spreading like butter
on the green hills,
and not doing anything about
the red blood staining the Square
they named Tian An Men,
Gate of Heavenly Peace.

Cowhead, Newfoundland
1989

Marisa Anlin Alps

MARISA ANLIN ALPS, born in 1970 of Chinese and Dutch descent, grew up on Quadra Island, B.C. She has her B.A. from Simon Fraser University and currently works in the book publishing industry. Her poetry has been broadcast on CBC radio and also appears in *Breathing Fire: Canada's New Poets* (Harbour). She lives on B.C.'s Sunshine Coast.

Chinese 5 Spice

My mother's hands smell of ginger
traces of sesame oil, Chinese 5 spice
the colour of miso, her long fingers
sift through the black mushrooms and
vegetables piled on the kitchen counter.
Shaping our meals with necessity,
garden soil and clay caught beneath
her nails, she washes her artist's hands
before she digs out the rice pot and
pours herself a glass of wine, sips
it as she stirs and simmers,
scented steam rising to greet the light.

My father's hands are wide and
lined with rough work, his fingers
blunt, stained with nicotine, the
coarse red hairs burnt short
near the nails. They smell of the sea,
salt ropes and diesel engines, of the
sails stored in the forepeak.
The other woman, my mother
says of *Carlota*, her sleek lines
hug the ocean like a lover,
moving with the wind in rhythm.

My father's best dish is eggs and toast,
but he relishes my mother's meals
like a gourmet, serving up lavish compliments,
recreating them in air—their flavours,
spices, aromas—they are closest to his
heart and heaven. He touches her hand and
murmurs *Mei Mei* before his half-finished
plate calls him back to earth.

This is how I see them together, here at the table.
Hands joined, the dark and the pale,
my mother's black hair, my father's red
my brother and I a blend of their own
particular recipes: a trace of her epicanthic fold,
a dash of his freckles, a hint of her oval face,
a seasoning of his wide shoulders,
a shade of her brown skin.

After the Wedding

The first time I realized I was Chinese
I was seventeen, travelled east
to Toronto to celebrate my cousin's
marriage, the sole relation
from my branch of the family tree.
I'd never seen so many of my relatives
in one place, their unknown
faces swirling before me
and everyone there was Chinese.

Suddenly it hit me and I knew
I was too (or at least half)
a surprise since I've been everything else
for so long.

My mother says she feels more Canadian
than anything else, but perhaps we moved
to the island pockets of the west
coast to emulate her island childhood, a hint
of possibility in the Caribbean accents
slipping so easily around me, a little
like those split leaf plants
my grandmother smuggled into Trinidad,
the ones that grew, flourished
took over a whole corner of her lovely
garden and yet, I felt white
for the first time in my life, different
still from everyone around me, especially
during dim sum in Toronto's Chinatown
an intense experience with tripe and
chicken feet and the wonder
of what was not said.

After the wedding, long and noisy tables
filled the banquet hall like sunflowers
pushing toward the centre of the dance
floor, couples whirling around the chairs.
My cousin asked me to dance but I was shy,
eyes downcast. *How did he see me?*
The flowers scented the air like wine,
voices like music, while others
flew I sat there on the edge, wonder pouring
from me, distant from the centre
I did not feel much, but I thought
I am Chinese
horizons shrinking
and changing before my eyes
a second wedding taking place
within me, two
inheritances exchanging vows.

Calligraphy Lessons

"Hold the brush like you have an egg in your palm," Mr. Pang said to me and I tried, cross-eyed with concentration. Once a week after my dance class my mother and I would squeeze into this small room off Little Panda and with a half-dozen others try to please Mr. Pang: ink on our fingers, paper like dry leaves, the colour of sticky rice. The stiff hairs of bamboo brushes turned soft from resting in our shallow water dish (my characters were always stunted and unsure, not what he wanted, long fluid brushstrokes) he taught me how to write my Chinese name one—two—three no! don't stop mid-stroke! 安 林 trees and peace.

I never did learn calligraphy, never discovered anything but my name, and later I would mourn this loss, would want to own this skill, hang it on my wall, framed in silk and weighted. I don't think my mother learned either, and my father and brother stayed home.

In Chinatown the waiters talked to her in Cantonese, and although my mother understood as little as I did, she always knew what to order, what was inside the rice flour dumplings, the sweet red surprises, brushstrokes tilting and scenting the air, hundred-year-old eggs staining her hands.

Following the Way

I
The ways are different
doors opening, closing
"A More Open China Awaits You" in the bid
for the 2000 Olympic Games
eyes stare and disappear to the tasks
before them.
My aunt has moved to Beijing
reclaimed her heritage, she proudly announces
her tall, lithe frame betraying her
northern origins.

She walks quickly through the crowds
easy to follow, her face Chinese
her voice and clothes speak foreigner
in this distant land
not lost among the streets choked with
bicycles and bodies, her navigation sure
learned in two years' time:
she bargains respectfully, with pride
boards buses with ease
takes Mandarin in small painful doses
from a neighbour upstairs, lives with the red
Beijing dust that coats her clothes like
she was born to it, says
I have learnt the Chinese way.

II
Generations of forgettings live
in Tiananmen Square.

In the April sun
red flags wave in the silent spring breeze
children chase their kites

following the crisscrossed tiles
and the little red birds and dragons swoop
toward the ground, nearly
striking the sad peasant men
who look for work, patiently
hovering over their belongings like flies.

We pose for pictures in front of Mao
and the Forbidden City, stand in line
for a glimpse of the great man himself
slightly swollen and embalmed in crystal
his mausoleum set beside the
Great Hall of the People.

Vendors frame the square
with carts full of film, golden Buddhas
Mao buttons, booklets and
the red, red flag of China

the ghosts are here still
in the stillness that shivers
through the throngs, in the afternoon
shadows, a slight pause in time, a glance upward
at the kites dancing
and singing in the wind.

III
Six thousand steps are carved
into the rock of Tai Shan, a great
grey snake winding to its distant peak,
each one made centuries ago by
human hands, the result as graceful
as the calligraphy etched
on the mountain side, reaching
toward the sky.

Midway, my aunts decline the climb
in favour of the cable car
     with only three thousand steps left

I pass heavy burdens
bricks, baskets of eggs balanced
on the shoulder, swinging in pendulum
rhythm with the men who carry them
young women climb the mountain
in high heels, and older ones also
falter on their small bound feet
families carry their children, rest
and leave money for the mountain gods
whose small red shrines, scattered
with the confetti of coins
decorate the steps like wild flowers
they ensure our safety as we make the
pilgrimage to this sacred mountain
whatever our temple might be.

On Heavenly Street I find
an arch of sky above, a hint
of other mountain tops far below
the way lined with vendors
a child lights a wand of incense for the
god of azure cloud, its musky
smoke joins the others burning
I go back and complete
the climb for the camera, my aunts
capturing my moment of triumph
as I finish the ascent
all history bearing down
behind me.

Blossoms

Any piece of fruit will suffice, as long
as it is savory and fragrant, golden and glowing
in the hot afternoon sun. Thirst
is important too, and need. I have seen all
of these in an unfurling flower
at a finger tip, a peach ripening to
a sweet age, an old beggar bent with hunger.

Once the pit is planted, a sprout springs up
so swiftly there is no forgetting, no eyes
for anything but this unexpected flowering.
First, leaves appear like smoke, all grey
green and light, faint pink blossoms
blaze along the branches in a consuming fire.
Before long the tree is taller than a grown
man, its trunk strong and sturdy,
sustaining the weight of ages. It bears
fruit so luscious years from now you will
still be crying for a taste.

Afterwards, there is emptiness and it isn't a trick
of light. Even the birds won't see your harvest
disappear, its sweet perfume scenting
the wind like song. Your heart torn apart,
cut in two by some great hand—nothing is worth
this loss.

Also known as "The Peach Tree." Other versions of this Chinese fairy tale feature
different fruit—from pears to starfruit—but all variations possess a greedy merchant
who refuses to share his wares with an old beggar man who is a supernatural being
in disguise. A good Samaritan buys a piece of fruit for the poor man, who eats it
with gratitude. After he finishes it, he plants the pit and a fruit tree begins to grow
instantly. Within minutes it is bearing fruit and the beggar man gives it all away.
The greedy merchant is so busy watching the spectacle he doesn't realize he has been
robbed until all the fruit is eaten and everyone has left.

The Empress' Feet

Strong and wide, flat as a
a hand and twice as long, her feet
were created to grip the earth.
They take her wandering
at night, all fourteen inches
restless, striving
to keep her moving through
dimensions.

These feet want her to see
the world, battle tigers,
encounter dragons who will squeeze
her in their coils, hiss their tongues
in her ear, bring shivers of delight;
they carry her.

Look, there she moves through
the market, testing the tiny crab apples
with her thumb. Now she sweeps
by the rice paddies, the murky
water underfoot whispers *shhhhh*.
Passing by a skirmish, she stops to
pole a bandit, place a well-aimed kick.
She climbs jagged peaks, her robes
reflecting all the colours of the sun;
the sleepy young men who are working
in the fields think she is the sunrise
against the mountains.

The empress dreams of the places
she will grasp with her
toes, searches for the pieces

cut from her. Not even chains
can bind her, these small feet trail
golden links, nine inches travelling
in shadow.

This Chinese fairytale explains one source for the Chinese custom of foot binding.
According to the tale, many hundreds of years ago, Chinese women had feet larger
than their husbands', and the longer they were, the more desirable. One empress had
feet fourteen inches long and she was seen as the most beautiful woman in the land;
her one fault was that she walked in her sleep and had terrible dreams. The empress
realized her sedentary day-to-day life left her powerful feet very restless, and this is
why her feet kept her walking at night. The emperor had nine inches cut from her
feet to stop her evening travels; afterwards, all noble women in the land were
ordered to have their feet bound so they would not have feet larger than the
empress.

Sean Gunn

SEAN GUNN, a former director of the Vancouver Chinese Benevolent Association, is a founding member of the Asian Canadian Writers' Workshop. As well, he composes for and performs in the Asian-Canadian musical ensembles Raw Silk and Number One Son. His music has been soundtracked for the video *Chinese Cafés in Rural Saskatchewan*, and the films *Moving the Mountain* and *Fishbones*. He has been anthologized *in Gum San Po, Inalienable Rice, Asianadian, Many-Mouthed Birds, Collected Voices*, and *Millennium Messages*.

assimilation

by any means
bleach out your jeans
and when they fade
you've got it made

and you wonder where the yellow went
when you brush yourself with permanent
brighter than bright
whiter than white
ninety-nine forty-four one hundred percent
and you wondered where the yellow went?

your ideal date
the great playmate
thigh high pie
in the sky
centre spread
across your head

oh mirror, mirror on the wall
who is the fairest, beneath it all?

and we wondered where the yellow went
when we brushed ourselves with permanent
brighter than bright
whiter than white
ninety-nine forty-four one hundred percent

by any means
bleach out your genes
and when they fade
you've got it made.

Orientation #1

in the world today
Chinese
are people
who live in China

on the local scene
Chinese
are adjectives
that modify people

And Then Something Went

click
da-da da-da dah dah
yeah steve
okay steve
right away steve
can I shine your automatic steve
click click
criminal like man with no culture
very difficult to find true identity
gee pop
why don't you let me solve a case sometime
number one son like a blind shao lin priest
must acquire power of vision
here
suck fortune cookie
click click
and when you snatch pebble from my hand
little number one grasshopper
I still suck fortune cookie
click click
now ree potato chip
click click
every day sammy tong houseboy
one day he find no peter
sammy tong shoot self in head
click click
beep beep
and the light at the other end of the tunnel
(of course)
is an oncoming freight train
(ofay trainus)
beep beep
click click
bok-bok
bok-bok

let's see
it's the ping-pong wizard
kicking the ass
of the man–I'm–glad
no wait a minute
up in the sky
it's a bird
dropping no
it's a
gregory peck playing ping-pong with chairman mao
bok-bok
bok-bok
and over there watching on the sidelines
it's suzie wong
galloping off
into the internal rising sunset
with william holden
'cause he uses commands
bok-bok
bok-bok
click click
beaver
it's almost the end of the show
I think it's about time
for our weekly
man to boy talk
gee pop
I thought you were inscrutable
click click
ancient chinese secret
calgonite
click click
hey chinaman
hey you
chinaman
what are you doing playing these here parts
I am *bok guey* come

in search of my long lost
brother the reason why I shave my head
is so that I can say
etcetera etcetera etcetera
click click
ah so
what's his name
goddamn lincoln mercury
what's his name
I said goddamn lincoln mercury
click click
kamikazes at 12 o'clock high noon
bam bam pow pow
kill the japs
bam bam pow pow
boys boys
glen
why don't you take your friend sean
outside to play
okay let's play cowboys and indians
I'll be the cowboys
no I want to be the cowboys
oh yeah
my daddy was the cowboys and your daddy was the indians
bam bam
pow pow
bam bam pow pow
click click
leo remon
click click
and what do you think
about carnations
well actually merv
I think I'd like to make a comeback
as a hunchback chinese dwarf
click click
and now for the secret square

tell me
what country
is known
as the homeland of the flat chest
click click click
but mister eddie's father
one hundred million miracles
is bullshit
my back is still wet
click click click
fuck you paladin
heck gai shee
we
have gun
will travel
click click click
don't shoot till you see the whites-click-click
bam bam pow pow pow
bam bam click click
bam click click
click

Bok guey: white devil (slang for white man)

Heck gai shee: eat chicken shit

Jamila Ismail

JAMILA ISMAIL is third generation colonial (b. 1940 Hong Kong), whose mazes have included Chinese-Indian/Anglo-French, 'race'/school, Cantonese-Urdu/English, Muslim/Catholic, gender/sex, Asian/Canadian, friends, family, roots (aerial, square, Qb). And so forth. Jam's lived in India, Hong Kong, Canada, YVR/HKG, and taught in British Columbia. Publications include *Sexions* (1984), *From Diction Air* (1989), *From Scared Tests* (1991), *(Translit-* (1997), and (with Jasmelie Hassan) *Jasmelie-Jamila Project* (1992).

school, rowdy starlings

tell   strangers
her   heritage
did   kin   there
shame her askew

repeating bird trills
by baqfuq flyover
'he wants only results
don't be insulted'

prose is . . . gossip
they're sayin' in trahna,
[ont.]   he'd said
she'd said

               flailily fetched
sidestep .   notch eye
new cement stairs !
alert young grasses !

look say

in dry month   much leaves   are caving
sound's having to relay scene
picket gate blue
                          a toy soldier's house
she did say 'you   are a tireless worker'

from garbage can where cut vine peeps
   strawbroom dips to shadow lawn
            wheel below barrow
                  —eye—

      sweet cicely turrets   'hi lovage, greeet!'
      beamier poppies   connote butterfly
as, cairn of small stones   butts square chimney pot
            as chopsticks pick off slugs

                  one sec

            nocturne .   e-e motion .

ghosts

                  prairie colouring ditch

      say 'light'   see single

      wed tumbled out of lark

      marble sky from night grass lain

      now dearly beloveds,

                        untie the sheaf

            (caught

translit–

              eration can be rather sub rosetta (make
that sub rashid)   look say   one sec   e-nigh   king
caught   all of a sudden (so it seemed) the british word
for *guy dan fa* irretrieved, tippy tongue

: well, so when her sister was doing her hair — 'do you
want it more *been* [flat],' she asked, tugging at the
plaits, 'or less *been*. . . .'   they giggled. she'd been
feeling pretty down at the mouth. weeks of rush to finish
the prototype for the software conference & what !? she
dreamt last night she served some thin vegetarian stew, with
celery. anxiety about salary cutback? 'celery . . . ,' her
mother mused. 'that's *kun lik* !' she twigged. 'you're
giving them your strength, your industriousness.' it never
occurred to her she'd dream in cantonese. 'ma !' she
blushed.

: in lit hillside colossus of aquaria   gigantic fish
moves plain silver black slow, its body filling tank

   in tank below, shelled headless prawn, leviathan of
sashimi hangs diagonal

   some will sometime soon read,   swimming treadmill
journalists & writers out on a limbo   like a single carp

old girl

you wanna bite a bun'

thus trevor minced)

across cross walk

neat blonde seemed

to be sussin' out

the parenthesis

short cuts
down steps
sweet bits

Dancing With Whooo ?   'd be trans

–lateable   'you

were seen eating in the streets,   in public !

singing out loud, like a . . . hick . .

feeling, as she watched white swirl above wedgewood blue while
toothbrushing baking soda into the carpet to deodorize it of the pee her
brother upset from the jeremiah when the security alarm rang through the
house the morning she slid open the balcony door, as if she were in a
window seat by the toilets looking down at clouds

forked root, djinn sang

ar thes eys soon to really never bus by   colour chips of
lai tak chune   flora ravined under flyover & bonsai'd
from highrise – '& how is your e-nigh?,' asked the radio,
tweaking a smile from cocktail of loniten, concor, ticlid &
cozaar.   for the King *Kingkingkingkingking M'Loc* was
winning the day against King *King Duckmy* as for what
hyphenation said to hymenation ('speaking in exchange for
anonymity') . . . last year, his dreams ran out of money.
now astronomy asks, should pluto be a planet . hmm . . !
dervish of bauhinia sniffed, replacing crown.
                                        packed up his
totipotence, did westward ho, & dashed off, leaving divi-
for what nation, dar- ?? landclaims both sides of pond. a
barely watered kettle *boings* over heat, north of 60. friable
urban gold, november leaves, loonily taxed. chinese & urdu
calligraphy black over road cracks.   you'd think, that's
tramwheels squealing into the depot at but it's times square
now on russell,   or alongside kennedy town abatoir, now
parking lot.   mais, canadarm de famille, e-coute, that's a
sound of the working fjord: burrard inlet.   with steeps of
greig scaled by   soyla isakovski, shelagh rogers was saying.
incroyable, that love could be a thing of ice in the veins,
spooky cryogen   no, it's cracked soap, positions left
unattended, bed alone, meals by on lok, dents & wear in
sofas empty of children, ,, aahhhhh   demoral !! he swore
so was sent to hospital for, he said, an anagram   exact
change turnstiles   in the aisles of northern spice   where
crows lunch on lawn   as seedy sunflower hours above
filigree of cosmos

Lydia Kwa

LYDIA KWA was born in 1959, in Singapore, the year that country gained independence from British Colonial rule. She came to Canada in 1980 to begin psychology studies at the University of Toronto. Since then, she has lived and worked in Kingston, Calgary and now Vancouver. She is a clinical psychologist as well as a writer. She has been published in various literary journals and anthologies, including *Many-Mouthed Birds* (Douglas and McIntyre). Her first book of poetry, *The Colours of Heroines*, was published by Toronto's Women's Press in 1994. The excerpts in this anthology have appeared in a 1999 issue of *Tessera,* as well as in an art catalogue, *Imaginings,* published through the Charles H. Scott Gallery, featuring the art of Ed Pien. *Suite of Hands* is a long poem-in-progress, of which eight excerpts appear here.

excerpts from SUITE OF HANDS

the left hand wants to write a feeling
of crushed, and going against

wants to unfurl
large as the voice singing

murmurs   to rhythms of the heart
hesitates at the sound of crying

In a dream suite, she realized she was without hands. The arms were there, familiar, easy, so that some part of her routine intelligence insisted on the truth of hands. Her eyes saw them, but they existed only as phantoms without the will to search for occupation.

While wandering through the first room, she sensed grief creep into her, one memory stretching into another. Tenderness a fleeting pulse from the centre of her chest. She glanced at a small dark table in the far corner, at its blue glass bowl choked with apricots, their skins fresh and waiting.

The sight of vulnerability.

But I didn't believe in my own touching, she whispered at the ash-grey walls, suspecting someone would hear her. Someone she might bruise with her hands, if she still had them. Someone walking around in a different dream suite, whose own mind had erased some other aspect of the body's original freedom.

Soon I'll know myself from having lost, losing until there's nothing left. She imagined each body she had stroked and rejected, until the memories ached at her wrists.

from a lake of dreams, quiet midnight
this hand is a hawk riding air

settles its wings over a memory
devil weapon of fine bones and muscle

What she had read in a book picked off the shelf of a bookstore. The quote entered now through the deeper door of sleep, and stood solitary in the shadows of the next room.

"There are the raised arms of Desire, and there are the wide-open arms of Need."

In the corner of dark mahogany panels, she squatted as if waiting for the train, the seventy-two hour one from Xian to Urumqi, as if it were ten years ago, that first seduction of an unknown journey. She squatted to listen better to the woman pacing the floor above her. That creaking presence, anxiety seeping through rhythm. Until the beat of that other's life paced in her mind, heavy and measured.

It was a man who wrote that: the primacy of Desire, the spontaneous gesture of Need. *Nothing thinks as clearly as the body.*

She raised her arms up to the ceiling, trying to reach the woman who paced, who knew nothing of this quote. How could she bruise this truth past the boundaries of her guarded life?

In a different dream, there was the meaning of light and air. Laughter, long before there had been reason to forget the beauty of apricots in a blue bowl. In a different dream, the woman above her existed in the same room as her, also squatting to wait for trains.

She was still, feeling the impending journey travel towards her, from the feet up.

a memory of the father's hands
beating at the heart

the kind of crushing
they were capable of

a memory of the mother's hands
crying with failure

The red room. Large, and echoing, a hall. Without the pretence of paintings or photographs. Frames left hanging after theft.

She looked out of a window, and in the distance at the edge of the world, there was a vision. It travelled towards her, slow as a breath exhaled. She walked out of the room onto the dusty streets. A walled city, yellow bricks carrying sunlight in their pores, a hundred feet high.

The loneliness, not knowing how long she would need to stay within those walls. Searching for something she wasn't aware of.

I will send her a letter. Reconciling herself to this sojourn. Thirty more paces, she arrived at the edge of a courtyard, defined by a low mud wall. Warriors, all men, in sea green breastplated armour and helmets. Their arms united in sweeping the solid arcs of defence.

She recognized the moves, the muscled art. She turned to address the feminine man, *I am familiar with this, but it is the ornamentation of temples I'm more interested in*. As if to say to him, that was the meaning of her search.

She raised her head and nodded to indicate what she meant. Behind the warriors, a low temple roof. Paler than the breastplates, a faint turquoise border of ceramic reliefs, curls and waves, ancient secret.

while silent, the left hand daydreams of
magicians and fire-eaters

reaches out
still believing in flight

The ceiling of the dream turned from red to midnight blue, then faded to grey. She was standing in a corridor, uncertain of where she was, this slim fragment of an unknown house. No windows, yet bars of light travelled across the walls on either side, as if urging her on.

The dreamer knew she was travelling, but not how long she had been sleeping. With tiredness so complete it captured her in its languid net and delivered her back into that dull ache. *It was her mouth that bruised me*, an invisible scar lodged between her breasts while her arms had been raised over her head, crossed at the wrists with the grip of a purple scarf.

She reached out to feel the light. Tracing with her fingers, as if decoding a secret message. *Corridors always lead to rooms*. If she walked on, eventually there would be a return. To a time when desire was full with its own restraint, when her hands had chosen to submit, laughing at the semblance of passivity.

Tenderness at the heart of her torso. Nothing could protect her now, not even fear.

The quote used in the fourth section is taken from Roland Barthes, *A Lover's Discourse*.

Fiona Tinwei Lam

FIONA TINWEI LAM was born in Paisley, Scotland in 1964 and emigrated to Canada with her family four years later. She has lived, worked, and/or studied in Kingston, Toronto, and Ottawa, acquiring three university degrees and plenty of life and work experience. She was raised and is now based in Vancouver. Her work has been published in *Descant, The Literary Review of Canada, Canadian Literature,* and Elizabeth Harvor's collection, *A Room at the Heart of Things* (Véhicule, 1998), as well as *The White Wall Review, The New Quarterly,* and *Bite.*

Mourning

At dusk, they invade the mirrors,
masked in sympathy.

In the kitchen, women flutter,
moths trapped in a jar.
Over the clink of teacups, their voices hum
about biopsies, medicines, comas.

The child huddles outside her mother's room,
a porcelain sentry.

A cry tears through the dark cocoon.
A flurry of women rush in
with smothering murmurs.

The child clasps her knees,
her heart mute.

Absentee

A folded square of thin white paper
from my mother to my teacher
justifies an absence.
He reads it, stillness taut inside me.
Something almost focuses.

The day comes, they wake me,
dress me in filmy black polyester,
a blouse made for a grownup.
I wait to know how to feel.

We are placed in a wide car
that smells of shoe polish,
an unspeaking family
face to face.

When we arrive at the Chinatown church,
people are expecting us. They stare at me
as if I've had an accident.

Dark-suited bodies in the pews
whispering Cantonese,
muffled chords from an electric organ,
floral bowers up front,
and a big box.
The singing trudges. Something long
comes out of the minister's mouth.

We are lined up by the door to cry,
receive people's apologies
for something they didn't do.
My eyes will not participate,
they don't remember how.

Some murmur before they pass,
aren't you brave.
My grandparents press their lips tight—
they raised her wrong,
unfilial child.
Others wonder
didn't she love her father?

When we return,
we close ourselves
into our rooms.

Alone, I wait to feel God.
Night gapes.

Cemetery on Boxing Day

Crows hop
staccato over the dead,
a sprinkling of commas.

Their heads bob.
Beaks pluck
the remnants of ritual:
stubs of incense,
rice lumps,
an orange.

Over my father's grave,
I listen, rapt,
for the light lift of their wings.

At Christmas time, many Chinese families leave food for the dead by family
members' graves.

Camouflage

outside, pacing fury,
a plywood door
prepares to buckle:

inside, a legless bed floats
docked against a wall,

medusas in the wallpaper's
clumped foliage peer
into an empty shag sea.

a narrow closet,
innards jumbled—
woolly hems, boots, and
a twelve-year-old.

her crouched silence.
she pretends to be
a shoe.

Faith

You are seeing yourself then—
ten years old and never grateful,
your dad teaching you
how to swim on your back.

Why do you panic?
The edges of the water
like poison lapping
into your ears and nose, the sinking
anchor of your hips, the way

the water wants you.
You must trust
his hands will save you.

But you don't.
You're supposed to.
Why don't you?

This is the only time
he will touch you,
the only time
he will teach you anything.

He is going to leave you
soon. In his coma,
he won't remember
how his hands held your head,
how you wriggled out

of his grip, rushing
to clutch concrete.

Narcissus

your lanky grunge adonis
his warhol locks so
darkly rooted

his salvation army garb
a noble display of
trust-funded poverty

his gaze fixed
upon the aesthetic
of his every jerk and waver

his kisses like velvet leaves
limbs like supple shoots
of poison ivy

doe-eyed spontaneity
when he murmured
he fucked you unintentionally

his last spurts of milky devotion
rinsed the very arteries
to your heart

Ring

you've told yourself
this ring is unlike
the ancient bandages
with their tight, wet grip
that crushed feet into lotuses,

unlike ribbed walls of bone
corsetting and fashioning
spine, womb, breath,

or the relentless
slide into another's name,

you tell yourself
this ring is
not an enclosure
not a boundary,
not a binding.

An Ordinary Place

the refrigerated air holds
a memory of salt, an alien sweat
soured by stillness.

tabled rows of sleek silver carcasses,
their upturned milky glares,
jaws caught in frozen snarls.

some sliced for display,
wedges of muscle fanned out on ice.
others, their defeat left whole.

carapaces stacked in murky tanks
sluggishly climb through
dreams of clear water.

we saunter in
to identify the corpse
for dinner.

Survivor

dedicated to Analee Weinberger

In this medicated world,
each morning is a mortician
preparing the dead for the undead
and the other way around.

Your mother's body, papery and hollow
on the white bed,
infected limbs blackening
under pale sheets,
eyes clouded with the distances
she has travelled
away from you. Now

she looks your way—who are you?
A shadow of a daughter
or only a voyeur? Everyone hovers
without wings.
Never soon enough, the doctor
injects his antiseptic sympathy.

You've smoothed her past two years
into certainty—black clothes, a burial plot,
lists of names to phone,
your own life stored
just beyond reach.

She cannot know this,
reduced to
pain, no pain.

Perhaps this is the day
everything will end,
begin.

Examination

You are splayed like a specimen
under fluorescent lights.
The doctor's fingers
rummage in your body
as if it were a broken toaster.

You talk about who hurt you
to this white-coated confidant
you've just met.
His metal tools neatly
aligned on a metal tray,
his hands almost glowing,
opaquely unreal
in their plastic gloves,
his glances of polite concern—
everything so carefully sterilized.

Waves of footsteps,
rattling stretchers and carts
wheeled on endless linoleum,
absent doctors being paged,
someone crying
down a labyrinth of corridors,
all sounds swabbed,
then wrapped in gauze.

An intern watches
your unravelling, his thoughts
dammed against a smirk.
You feel your vulva turning
into pussy.

The fingers snag a nerve.
Your eyes shut. You feel
theirs stay open.

Evelyn Lau

EVELYN LAU is the author of *Runaway: Diary of a Street Kid* (HarperCollins, 1989), *Fresh Girls and Other Stories* (HarperCollins, 1993), *Other Women* (Random House, 1995), and *Choose Me* (Doubleday, 1999), as well as three collections of poetry: *You Are Not Who You Claim*, *Oedipal Dreams*, and *In the House of Slaves*. She is presently at work on a collection of essays. She lives in Vancouver.

Coming Home

coming home, you counted one person dead
for every year you were away in Singapore
eating rice and vegetables, standing by the side of the road
where the thinness of the people swelled to fill the streets
under a hood of heat.
you returned with a camera and a pair of socks slowly stained
the colour of your shoes, expecting nothing,
not the rain that lay like glass outside the motel window,
or the cold through your cotton shirt. seeing nothing
but one friend hanging by a leash from the bridge,
puffy as a purple fig.
listen, you said in the parking lot outside,
the silence, listen to it, and I saw it cut you
with its high horrible delicacy, its vicious thinness,
so much silence to chatter you could hardly stand it.
so this is my country, you said, and your eyes pulled tight
and your laughter forced sound after sound in the air.

Green

and already the leaves have arrived,
my doctor, that blur of green you spoke of four years ago
thickened while you sat, spread in your chair in the sun,
children scuffing bicycles down the alley to the grocery store.
it was not really green, you said, but rather
a haze of green, a fog of green,
a thought of green you could only call light.

I awoke from a dream panicked
thinking I'd missed the arrival of the leaves.
a landlady was walking from room to room,
each one barren and small and filled
with the sound of typewriters. there was a view
of a beach in the distance, the encroachment of a wave
like a finger, spray hitting the empty shore,
a foreign beach the colour of dust.
the trees were black arms holding up the sky,
crookedly. along the sidewalk in front of the building
that fine mist, that vague rain of green had gone,
and the branches were bent with a new burden of leaves.

four years ago we had word-associated this thought of yours,
this green that wasn't there,
back when mysteries were still abundant
and could be uncovered. yesterday everything was plain
and unbudging as a jug sitting in the sun.
the beach was the colour of your shirt, sand,
the colour of your face new to the sun.

in the morning there was no way of telling
if the leaves had come, since there were only buildings,
every room a bleak room. the phone rang loudly

while you, my doctor, went hunting in the park for the hint
of green, the cloud of green that was still mysterious
and therefore solvable, the green that failed to exist.
it breathed along the backs of your thick white hands
as the phone rang in my chest
without a sound, and you groped further and further
down the beach with the voice of the sands.

Projections

and it may be that you learned nothing, it is possible
to be exhausted from this sleep, to remember nothing
except the oldness of his body reflected
in a restaurant mirror, retreating from you,
shoulders bladed in the blue sweater
hands dropped down in defeat or depression.
how narrow his face looked, blackened with strain,
the eyes false and mirroring, green stone,
green as water, shifting.

that last night he feasted
on the unveiling of a year of lies,
the membrane of delusion lifted away in his fingers
like a graft of skin, like a skein of silk,
like wings.
the lies you promised to tell with your hands folded
safely in his, while the walls of his office
blushed slowly pink over the months as if shamed.
hour after hour the fog of pills shut him out
till his face was a father's face, healer,
destroyer, lost in its grip of private darkness.

he said he had never met anyone
so tragically like himself.
in thirty years, who could say?
meanwhile he handed you secrets like presents after a journey,
the broken men, the wounded healers that so delighted
and frightened him, the simian men who lectured
at the front of conference rooms with calloused eyes.
theirs were names that rhymed and rolled
off the tongue, you harvested the sick convulsive sweetness
of his secrets about the doctors with their women patients
their curious fingers.

but before long it seemed that something ended,
the light rusted, you rose dazed from a year as if
from a long sleep and dreams of love,
dreams twisting into nightmares.
and there was the silver afternoon, the metal plate of the day
tearing aside the blanket of your Oedipal dreams,
tearing him away till the day was dull and the room empty
and the sky unmoved. and you sat in the middle of your bed,
not a child, with Daddy grey and bent in the bathroom mirror
looking terribly confused, his fingers tapping ten anxious thoughts,
old as myth.

Room of Tears

you showed me pictures of mollusks
and sea urchins, some spike, some flabby
as wombs, the sand a shifting floor.
you were the fifth person to enter the room of tears
in centuries, this cave named
for stalactites and stalagmites worn
to the shapes of teardrops.

we talked until you were ready for sleep,
brass bed and black pyjamas.
your body straight in sleep, sheets pulled to chin,
had the blurred curves of a mummy in the British museum,
wrapped in bandages the colour of parchment.
yet your face was alive as a lamp,
pupils wide to take in the remaining light.

it took nights to learn your body,
the way your lips pushed together in pain
or joy, the sounds you made with your mouth gagged
when threats and whips slammed the wall above your head,
what colour horror painted your eyes.
your fingers furled and opened like soft creatures
underwater, an Enya tape on the stereo
and behind my eyelids the English countryside flashing by
the way it did that spring
from the back of a sports car, endless green,
and lambs who dropped tails like feces on fields
bordering the stones at Avebury.

it was the silence
of the deep sea you loved, the cut of the coral,
the creatures that breathed with their bodies

as if their whole bodies were genitals, feeling, pulsing,
opening. tears fell
on your shoulders from the ceilings of caves,
and fish lit the water white
as happy brides.

The Lost Hours

in dreams where you walk I am a pale scar around your neck
a leaf twisting about your ankles, I am between the fingers
you rub together, betraying a desire to take notes
25 years of taking notes in analysis and the gesture comes to you
like a blink or a tense muscle.
I have kept the lost hours
the nights you thought I gave to needles
and the snowflake scatter of white pills
—they cause amnesia, you said, and the truth to come out—
your hands reached out gloved in softness to gather up
the babble of truth that slipped from my mouth in a rush
of polished stones, marbles.

you thought I'd lost hours like trinkets while you were busy
driving home through a blizzard of night
and a cold that stuck itself to you like a wet tongue
thrust against an iron gate in winter
you abandoned loneliness for an office party where you insisted
the nurses lined up to press their bodies against yours
I wonder what you wore?
your patients escaped through a black corridor with seeking hands
balleting around their faces
their hands fluttered art above the chair I fell into.
you pocketed the hours, I spent them freely
and walked with you into imaginary havens, saw you serious
with a sunken lip, saw that same lip grasping another
tasting of lipstick and tears and confessions.

I have held the lost hours in my own dry palm
I have sought them and it has been like looking for
something buried on a beach after dark, I have been looking,
combing back the hairs of the afternoon.
all your lost people thrum in the darkness of the night
I have had to learn to forgive each one

often they had delicate hair
the first whiff of defeat had been ironed into their clothes
already their eyes had gone.
why did you leave it so long?
the two Chinese lamps in your office held nothing back
the floor was awash with the layers of your suit, we were
struggling to learn something or to forget everything
beneath books by Freud and Havelock Ellis and some new
California psychologist.
you had written me into your appointment book with initials
that were not my own.
I counted the hours into my purse and wrote the important names
into a black book in the bathroom
and laughed all the way back down the long hallway to your office
because you were smiling where you stood.

The Smaller Life

it was a schoolgirl you wanted, with a still white face,
crossing the bridge between Eton and Windsor,
a peppermint girl swinging a bookbag,
the grey Thames under her feet,
the swell of stone under her feet. a striped schoolgirl
with tears the taste of grapes
and a body full of imaginings

but Peter in the chapel
with his curious clammy hands, those flint eyes
selected you from across the courtyard,
across three-quarters of a million pounds of stones and pebble,
by the Founder's Statue where you stood
on gold pieces. Peter with the moist eyes
took you behind the organ, up
triangles of stairs, where the boys' crosses hung.
outside, split sides of flint
shone like eyes in the courtyard, and on the Windsor bank
bluebells under every tree,
and statues with the stomachs of angels.

it's a smaller life now,
too narrow a life for the flourishing of words,
for the vines and accidental blooms of language
to overtake silence. while your wife
sleeps her voluptuous sleep, you sense how life has shrunk,
and your mouth droops like an unchecked eyelid,
a moment's unrecoverable banishment of self.

Kam Sein Yee

KAM SEIN YEE was born to Southern Chinese immigrants in Vancouver in 1967, the sixth of seven children. She grew up near Chinatown, took a B.A. in History from the University of British Columbia, and studied at Université Laval in Quebec. After working for a number of years for the "feds," she completed her nursing diploma at Langara College. Recently she spent a year in Malaysia, working with Battered Women's groups on a CIDA and Malaysian AIDS Council project. Her manual on teaching reproductive health is used in women's shelters in South East Asia. Previous credits include work in *Fireweed* and *Pediatric Nurses' Quarterly*. She currently edits a nursing newsletter, *Global Health Interest Group,* and works for the Registered Nursing Association of B.C. She is also working on her first novel.

When I dream I am my father

When I dream I am my father
I spend my days in the rice paddies,
wading up to my waist
my dark legs scarred with white lines
from long strings of leeches I have pulled off
weeping a little blood
as they release

I can catch small fish that tickle my feet
to eat later
when the sun is not touching every part of me
so that I taste the air and sweat and rice
and hunger
and moving mud beneath my feet

flies suck the moisture
from my face
that escapes from the rag
I use to tie my hat

as I stoop to cut
grasping firmly
and pulling up
and again
my rhythm
creates a shadow
that moves like
a swallow
over the water

there is no sound
but the insects
that move through the fields
like pieces of blue glass
thrown in the wind

And when I dream I am my father,
I am ten years old
going to school
to have my hands whipped raw
from a bamboo cane
with dust, thick like chalk,
from the road to the village
on my feet
that will not feel shoes
until they are sixteen

and so I stop
to catch
grasshoppers
to roast by the path
gently pushing the stick
through their soft green bodies
and watch their simple eyes
that look at me
as they turn black
and curl up with smoke

When I dream I am my father
I am sixteen
I am running,
I am running so that
I feel the blood in my ears
I am running and thankful
I am not a girl
whose breasts they will bind
down with rags
and hair they will cut off
so the Japanese will not rape her
when they find her
as they have found the rice
and the precious pig

I reach our house
the only brick home in the village
where I was born
my mother's sounds
filling the courtyard

the straw burns quickly
like the locust.
leaving the bricks
to fall and
mingle their red dust with white ash

I remember this
as I leave the plane
and see the Canadian flag
for the first time
a limp rag
frozen to a pole
in the Montreal snow.

My hands burn with remembered heat
as they touch the hands of
my grandfather for the first time.
Red and fleshy hands
that are cracked with spilt dry cleaning fluid.
I close my eyes
that I may breathe and begin.

Make a cradle for rice

It takes practice to make *jung*
to fill it with the right amount
of wet raw rice
yellow lentils,
pork belly and
tiny slivers of black leaves
from a flower with no name

ahh, the final crowning
with a
solid stem of
lup cheng

only buy Kam Yuen sausages
you don't listen to me

to take the dusty bamboo
leaves
saved and reused
a hundred times
so that

even after hot water soaking
fibres tear with an ounce too much
revealing a gaping hole
like an unclosed eye
no amount of string will hold it

hard rice falls
on the floor
on your feet
and apron

and now you have to throw away leaf
how come you so slow
how come you so stupid

one long strong leaf
making cradle for rice
an artful placement
of ingredients

make corner tight
like this
like this
how many times have I told you

two leaves to wrap and enclose
the whiteness
so much dexterity in just one old hand
that takes the white string
knotted every few inches

after you can tie the string together
and make ball
always save money
always save money

how swiftly and with strength
three leaves
become a perfect triangle
taut, tight
tie harder, tie harder
so that no rice may escape
from a six hour boil

it will feel nothing
but its
own final swelling

My knuckles whiten
as I tighten the cords that bind
like the iron lotus foot
when they cut off the toes
x-rays show warped metatarsals
necrotic and perfumed
with balms
and powders
bound tight and taut with knotted silk

no pain after the first cut
no bleed after one month
no feel after one year

so small, so theatrical
the layers of coverings
that end up in museums

put shoe on stove, that way remember
always fill up pot
more water, more water

I long to cover the lotus bud
with fresh bamboo leaves
to heal the cuts
with warm sesame oil
to plunge it into boiling water
so that it
may swell
deeply
again
into humanity

there is no need to cut the string
to open the steaming packet
it slides off the short end

remember, two strings, yellow bean
three strings, gan sui
save string, save string

the silk leaves pull away from the sticky rice
revealing, I know already
a perfect triangle
of
plump white flesh

Pierced Ears

my mother likes to feel my earlobes
and examine the
tiny perfect holes
made by a "professional"
for eight dollars
at the Bay

she gets this dreamy kind of look
in her eyes while
her fingers gently
rub the fleshy
pink flaps

the holes in her
sallow lobes
are elliptical
and loose

she tells me how her ears
were pierced

when she was thirteen
in China
how her mother
sat her up

on a wooden
stool in the kitchen
gave her
an unbelievable treat
a whole boiled chicken leg
to eat by herself
a dream come true

she tells me her smug
sisters stood by
and watched enviously as

chicken went into her mouth
smiled evilly because
they knew what happens
next

big sewing needle
this long
used for sewing sacks

of grain
heated in a pot of water
and a long red thread
attached to the end with a green bead
and suddenly holds her head
tight and jabs
the needle through
the ear
and wipes up some of the blood
which continues
to flow
and says
"now you can get married, you can wear
gold earrings"

I think about my mother's wedding night
to a man she barely knew

who would beat and curse her
for the next forty years
she might have wanted to
return the chicken leg

Spoon

to make rice porridge,
put a china spoon
in the pot, it will sink to the bottom

so in stirring
the spoon scrapes

your *jook* will
never burn

when my father's back was sore
mother took the china spoon
scraped
red smelly substance
until
his back became
straight lines of rising blood
but surface skin
remained unbroken
by the toothless spoon

sweaty effort
scraping so hard, for so long
required a cigarette and a beer
but eventually, it would end
this painful exercise

my mother could wash
her hands and rest
my father would be able to sleep
the spoon left unclean

Small Face

Face, a loaded word:
racist, bitch, liar, cock-sucking homo,
impossible to counter a self-hating jew
trite to say
face
controls your life
if it didn't, there isn't a drop
of ancestral blood

how much to bring to PoPo
impossible to measure
a family forever shamed
like the wrong café in San Francisco
forgotten cousin fifteen times removed or exhumed
from Grandfather's fourth concubine in Mexico

and they don't really run around like mad
waving gold American Expresses at pinky pearl.
You stinky girl, should know better

a real face is more subtle, cruel,
not you like now
not now, never better

so your wedding day face will circus contort
as you put on your face before your made up one
and drown it in
chrysanthemum tea ceremony
cup of life
rip it off
when your mother comes
to hang the heavy jade tire around your neck
and pull the gold rope tighter
you and then you, how beautiful,
your small little face, it is so
small face.

Larissa Lai

LARISSA LAI is a Vancouver-based writer and activist. In 1995, she was a recipient of the Astraea Foundation Emerging Writers Award. Her novel *When Fox Is a Thousand* was nominated for the Chapters/Books in Canada First Novel Award in 1996. Her writing has appeared in numerous exhibition catalogues, anthologies, and magazines including *Fuse, Rungh, Room of One's Own, absinthe, Kinesis, Bringing It Home: Women Talk About Feminism in Their Lives, Eye Wuz Here*, and *Many-Mouthed Birds*. She has recently returned from a ten-month stint as the Canadian Writer-in-Residence with the Markin Flanagan Distinguished Writers Program at the University of Calgary and is currently working on a second novel entitled *Salt Fish*.

amnion

embryonic bird
sleeps in its
translucent sac
dreaming its yolk
yellow origins the future
unfolding and spread of
destiny

a bird cannot speak
of what a bird does not yet know
when its foot bones
gelatinous soft
harden after hatching
it leaves dance tracks
in the sand

fish ball girl

fish ball girl offers
her cold package
one dollar only
i have the nerve
to bargain her down

wet floor naked bulb
her wan face hopeful
was this what we ran from?

uneven roundness
means handmade
white planets swimming
in hot soup
the flap and glitter
of swimming fish elided

is she the front or the maker?
between whose aching palms
were these morsels rolled?
i open my mouth
and pop one in
close my jaw
texture both tender and crisp
ideal flesh of some mythic beast
that neither sees nor bleeds
but sits in the dark factory
kneading with patient hands
docile or merely waiting?

upsidedown poem

it's been thirty years
since I've lain like this
knees on a chair
curled above head and neck
which rests on the ground
my body forms
a comma   *and*
or an inverted question mark

i didn't know
anyone could grant me
such grace
gravity tugging
the back of my skull
melting all sense of direction
and all fear
i didn't know
i could bring myself
to this place

who can call me
unnatural
in this position?
my mother knew me
this way first
when i slept like a snake
in her belly
unknown but
much imagined
an intimate stranger
poised between dream
and reality

after less than a year
of peaceful sleep
i fell
suddenly from grace
without wings
infinitely less than divine
threatening murder
and coated with blood
this was the first betrayal
but who was the perpetrator
she or i?

afterwards i walked upright
forgot the careful fingers
that traced
my limbs and veins
into being
forgot the dreams
and secrets
whispered into the convolutions
of my developing brain

my mother became preoccupied
rice rides blankets
while i stuffed my mouth
with language
pushed out the last remnants
of old memory

now she lives
half a continent away
and i know her only
disembodied through technologies
of distance
five-minute phone calls
and once-a-year
charter flights

if i curl here
remembering how heavy
i was
as a fetus
how without fear or knowledge
as though hanging asleep
in some ancient garden
could i return
to a place where stars
bloom at my feet
and the earth turns
like a distant satellite
below my head?

dispersing

an i ching poem

1. *dispersing*
to scatter clouds or crowds
what are we
if not water
floating free
of its resting place

2. *the king imagines possessing a temple*
the ideogram: person + borrow
grasping at the mist wisps
of dream
two women i no longer love
asleep
their faces
washed in tranquillity
a shower   hot rain
pummels
the top of my head
foot powder
a car window spilling
with clothes, books
a portable lamp

3. *gorge*
the streaming moment
ventures, falls, toils and flows on

4. *scatter*
the ideogram: strike + crumble
force of
how you didn't look at me
i wince
and fade

5. *radiance*
the ideogram: bird + weird
oil bright plumage
wet feather smell
chicken coop
chinaman
hey frank
buck buck bagaw

6. *tending towards the supreme*
the ideogram: rippling water
a grey stone
drops into lake
solid into liquid
concentric rings of
quiet want
internal oceans
rocketing heavenward

7. *exhaust*
the ideogram: cave + naked person
my monstrous mouth
dark eating   innocence
first love   first child
freakishness of not
understanding the shape
of beauty
expose my hunger
to the wind

8. *acquire*
the ideogram: go + obstacle
if you suffer too much
for what you get
does that make it
more worth having?
new world a blank

slate only when you don't
understand how old
the rivers

9. *situation*
the ideogram: person + stand
servants in their places
hong kong cricket club
now a park
where the filipina maids
gather on Sundays
once great
grandfather stretched
boy
as in hey boy!
another scotch and soda
would you
to steward
stretches into family
gathered round the lazy susan
tennis star grandfather
first chinese man ever to beat
a white man
on his own court
bosses the filipina maid

10. *dwell*
the ideogram: earth + persevere
through the cold dark
our feet wet in our boots
faces chapped rugged
friendly mr. pettigrew asks
you inuit?
earth plus persevere
through salt
on the road
in the hinges of doors

and axles of our red corolla
salt eats at the clockwork
of our hearts
nothing destroys iron
like its own rust

11. *centre*
the ideogram: field divided in two parts
out of love i give both parts to you
out of faith you return them

asian bird flu

one point three million chickens slaughtered
a ritual of blood less significant
than if it were human but still something
unholy, the slaughter a purification against disease
is it really the birds who are so unclean
in this dangerous ex
colony or is there something more fearful
that looms above us
and if so can we understand it in terms of chickens
asian bird flu the globe and mail calls it
glob and snob my sister
says derisively

asian bird flu and other epidemics from the far east
the financial pages say referring of course
to the recent collapse of the korean economy
world bank rushes in
armed with cash instead of guns

the bird can be slaughtered their useless bodies
buried in landfills
how will they spiral up to heaven
if no one burns them
and if the ancestors are there
to greet these dumb unlucky birds
will they eat them or
understanding their misfortune on earth will they
construct a few heavenly coops
feed them on stars and moon dust

and as for us, when all the chickens are gone
what shall we eat
what will pass our lips
what will fuel our hearts and hands
if not the bodies

of birds simple, stupid
too preoccupied with survival to understand how their dna
has betrayed them
how their blood coursing with mysterious disease
must now leave their bodies
the inscrutable, unnamable danger having already burst
rapid fire through their cells

and when we eat should we too be frightened
of how our blood might betray us
through the mysterious replication of alien cells
should we be frightened of the shapes
our bodies might take in the progress of disease
the shapes that already loom above us
heavy with blood and the stunned bodies of birds
insignificant except in the magnitude of their numbers
too small too miserable to care

Laiwan

LAIWAN was born in Harare, Zimbabwe, of Chinese origin. She emigrated to Canada in 1977 to leave the war in Rhodesia. She started the OR Gallery in 1983 and is an interdisciplinary artist and writer based in Vancouver. In recent years she has been researching the effects of technology on consciousness and perception. This second installment of "Notes towards a body" continues her exploration into the erasure of the "body" of race, class, gender, and sexuality along with cultural and geographical contexts within technological systems. Her first installment on this theme was published in the *Capilano Review* (series 2:24:1998).

notes towards a body II

1.

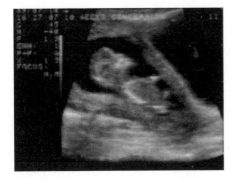

i am remembering the time i was not yet born
when there was no such thing as time
and no such thing as remembering

no, i am wrong
i remember, but not through memory

here in an image of being *not yet* in this world
a floating, bouncing, jumping shape closer to cyborg than human

a pixelated mass where i am a life of something else
of dancing lights without body

in a cramped, unfamiliar, freezing space
which could be purgatory, limbo, nowhere
everywhere

this couldn't be me
this being couldn't

i can no longer feel her. i ignore her as she always available yields.
mother, forgotten by a surge of inhumanity:
the one person who could know so well unconditional love
who could be my body of compassion
yields to forgottenness

i, waiting to be born become remembered solely by a frozen image
of a frozen time
of the not yet born
of the still being born
of the still being and the still born

of a still life in portrait
longing for body

2.

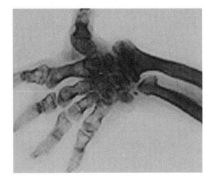

i am remembering mother's hands
no this is not hers she is not here
not a part of this

could this be my hand? could this be of my hand?

do we regret contributing to this most dulling of deeds
of removing life from being itself?

holding onto mother
before i was born fists clenched
fearing nothing but the invention of time and being named
named by image then frozen in space

compassion and memory and body
are shocked into silence
eliminated in the process

this couldn't be me
this being that couldn't

i remember, not through memory
i remember   mother feeding me

3.

my memory a body
remembering every crashing wave

how can i come to know unconditional love

when desire comes in waves, a push and pull effect
drowning in an unknown instigated by some karmic trick

i am going in, looking in
to see what i am made of

i once believed love originated from my mother's body
i once believed my body came from my mother's love

i once believed compassion could only come from remembering
this   my mother was my body

from where is the cause of my upheaval
this knotted gut
this gutted heart
this disheartened surgery of feeling?

outside of this condition, i am remembering unconditional love
in a body tremble or body sweat, i remember
gut feeling

4.

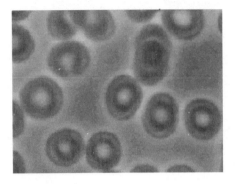

this is my body, this is my blood
no, i am wrong, this is a portrait of me

in all these processes
i have been searching for ways to bring some body back
mother, me or past and future lovers

i am remembering the stillness of this moment
which reminds me of when i once had to be reminded of mortality, of body,
of blood
of when i was reminded to be still

i look at her and remembering comes flooding back to body
blood rushes to circulate some kind of lightness
and day to day motion becomes derailed for this most invisible of flurries

still, i am breathing deep
so as to never neglect
what her body is telling me   what my body is telling me
without words, without gesture
not silent, but telling in a rush of catching up

never forget
how telling this is: this rashness of blood circulating some kind of insistence
circumnavigating unconditionally a desire to listen to this that so reveals

this image: this is my blood
outside of me because i had forgotten

how telling she is

Image sources:
Ultrasound image of foetus from the internet.
X-ray of hand from the Human Genome Project on the internet.
Bowel and intestine area from exploratory surgery of anonymous donor.
Blood cells of the author captured through an electronic microscope.

Leung Ping-Kwan

LEUNG PING-KWAN
grew up in Hong
Kong, and has been
writing since the late
1960s. He the author
of nine books of poems,
including the following
bilingual (English and
Chinese) editions: *City
at the End of Time*
(1992), *Foodscape*
(1997), *Clothink*
(1998), and *Travelling
with a Bitter Melon*
(forthcoming, 2000).
He has also published
six books of fiction,
one of which,
Postcards from Prague
(1990), won the first Hong
Kong Biennial Literary Award
for Chinese Fiction in 1991. His
books of criticism include *Books
and Cities* (1987), *Hong Kong Culture*
(1995) and *Cultural Space and Literature
in Hong Kong* (1996). He studied
Comparative Literature in U.C.S.D., and
has taught Cultural Studies and Creative
Writing in Canada and Hong Kong.

An Old Colonial Building

I.

Through sunlight and shadow dust swirls,
through the scaffolding raised-up around
the colonial edifice, over the wooden planks
men live on to raise it brick by brick, the imperial
image of it persisting right down, sometimes,
to the bitter soil in the foundation, sometimes finding, too,
the noble height of a rotunda, the wide, hollow corridors
leading sometimes to blocked places, which, sometimes,
knocked open, are stairs down to ordinary streets.

2.

Down familiar alcoves sometimes brimming
with blooms sometimes barren I go to xerox
glancing at the images caught in the circular pond,
now showing the round window in the cupola as duckweed drifting,
day and night caught in the surface, no longer textbook
clean, but murky, the naive goldfish searching
mindlessly around in it, shaking the pliant lotus stems
and the roots feeling for earth, swirling orange and white,
gills opening and leeching, in and out of the high window bars.

3.

Might all the pieces of ruins put together present
yet another architecture? Ridiculous the great heads on money,
laughable the straight faces running things. We pass in this corridor
in the changing surface of the pond by chance
our reflections rippling a little. We'd rather not bend;
neither of us is in love with flags or fireworks.
So what's left are these fragmentary, unrepresentative words,
not uttered amidst the buildings of chrome and glass, but beside
a circular pond riddled with patterns of moving signs.

The Leaf on the Edge

Sorry the food doesn't get to the leaf at the pond's
edge, still, you accept the homage due the beauties
at the centre, being the centre, leaf battlements and all,
reprising the regimens like an old regime. On the edge,
I'm nowhere in particular, a smoke-signal in a sandstorm,
a border legend, a plotless detail in the weeds of history.

Please don't make an imperial scene, or shout
anthems to the downpours; don't pretend, with the breezes,
to grant us our ditties. Have you ever noted a marginal leaf,
observed the veins converging like noisy streets,

that challenge your blueprints' rectangles? What about this?
Beneath the solemn appearances of the sacred blooms,
under water, roots grow together, new leaves furl in the heart.
Beneath the winds' quarrels, a hidden song needs other listening.

Seagulls of Kunming

Suddenly there you were, soaring
above Jade Lake, holding,
then heading straight up the sky.
My eyes filled with the brilliance of flight.
The light was all snow-white wings.
At the end of bleakest winter,
from instincts following warmth,
you make your great journey
to this town famous for its spring.

This is your happiness:
to find the good place.
As the sun returns
the days fill with perennial youth
winging and calling out
unbound joy in muscling the air,
in the freedom of flight.
During the hard days of the War,
merely somebody looked up from his shabby quarters
to find something splendid in the sky.
In their loud marches as well as in secret thoughts
how high their visions soared.

I lingered by the lake counting,
visiting the places where everybody held forth.
The campus was still haggard, Democracy Lawn knotted and rutty.
Memories were there somewhere, though
I couldn't help realizing there were fewer birds,
and those flew in broken circles.
One morning I got up to find you gone.
Was it a sudden chill?
Were you having to hide for a while?

Were you simply gone off again
in search of warmth?
Where would you build nests next?

Where was the air just right for soaring?
At what great shores
Would you next delight expectant eyes?

At West Lake

In "Nine Turns Bridge" I see, far off, a grove
of flat palms waving in the wind easily,
and I'd pick up my pen to show you how a West Lake tourist
goes in the crowds, picking his way by the pond
where flowers have spread out. I wasn't thinking of
classical diction, in spite of the famous dynasty costumes
on Ruan Gong Island, so famous for ancient pageantry.
This would have to be my story, full of twists and turns,
that trusts as we pass the old grove we'll come finally
to the undisturbed pond in the mind, take time freely there.
Next to the dried, yellow leaves are fresh, clean, red ones.
Picking up my pen I note immediately the faint
imprint of veined flowers—there are patterns hidden in the paper.
Why should I sully these with words? How shall I reveal
human changes across the context of flowers?
With each rubbing, elegant calligraphy becomes fainter.
The famous statues of the past go under to cultural upheavals,
and if not, down to graffiti. One follows the curves and hooks and twists
in the calligraphy and finds wounded figures, hurts for the injured words.
The old legends are still around, not as banally, though,
as the tenements that hoard the quiet beauty by the lake.
We walk "Nine Turns Bridge" and are no closer; whoever loves these flowers
must endure the mockeries of perfect distance. Fish-watchers realize
their gills and mouths are in feeding hands. "The Moon in the
Heart of Wave"
is only candles making tiny glares and large shadows.
Myths, ultimately, prove the discrepancies. I have to see you
wisely laughing at my dainty, elegant, floral designs.
Upheavals, graffiti, apartments, and smoke-stacks surround
West Lake now, the trees wave surely in some woe,
and the undersides of the ripples take away the moans.
The dry wind's wrist spreads the water's surface as if to write
this world's own sleek, lucid calligraphy.
In the mists and patterns of a horizonless paper lake we're like
accidental stains,
from fragmentary strokes left guessing at the whole script's life.

Soup with dried Chinese cabbage

A sudden stir, loud cheering, burst of applause
The Vietnamese man sings loudly into the microphone
We can't talk, so we concentrate on the soup of the day
Chinese cabbage cooked and then dried, and now in the hot soup
Simmering memories, brewing old tastes
In those fine days, under the sun they were dried, in moldy drizzles
Taken back into the house, tucked away amidst junks,
Mixed with the smell of years and dust,
A gift for visiting relatives, thrifty generosity,
In time pulled out, daring-cautious,
Along with the roots, for a long journey
To alien soil, roots snapped, fibre still entwined

The bride comes out, beside her the bridesmaid
Heavily made-up, in a *cheongsam* we find distantly familiar,
Embroidered with dragon and phoenix—another woman begins
To sing–is she the woman we saw just now in the car park,
Sitting on the sidewalk crying?
The MC, a man, speaks above the din, is he the one we saw just now in the
Grocery store run by the Cambodian of that Thai food take-out place
Amidst a jumble of junks?
Behind the noisy toasting, the glittering paper-cuts on the backcloth
Illuminate spellings of names. How to pronounce them?

The kids don't like this soup, funny taste
Last time I had such a soup—Sorry, I beg your pardon,
What did you say?—it must have been many years ago
Kids have no memory of moldy drizzles, they don't like
Dried Chinese cabbage, they complain about
This grotty restaurant in Chinatown, too many Asians
The food is salty (how do I explain to them the story of
Dried Chinese cabbage? Of yesterday's taste changing into the taste of today?)
Complain that the Vietnamese is still singing in the hall

We can't talk. Well, in a world so unfamiliar,
A certain way of life is all one could hang on to, I suppose
It's a wedding banquet after all, people look so happy
If only we could understand their language, if only we could, from the crinkled
Corners of their mouths, from those exciting lyrics, understand their song.

Eggplants

Vermicelli made from bean starch
Picked up with chopsticks, savoured
My tastebuds report: it is mixed with
Eggplants cooked to a mush

Memories surface, of the first time we met
Conversation drifted, we chatted about eggplants
I remember you said you grew up in Taiwan
Your dad was a Cantonese, your mum from Beijing
I forgot to ask how your folks cooked eggplants
Did you cook it first, leave to cool, and dress it with sesame oil?
Eat it with a hot, fish-flavoured sauce? Or have it Cantonese style—
Stewed fish with eggplants, stewed chicken with eggplants?

Isn't it amazing our thoughts all travel from food
To culture bonds, from reactions of the body and
Cravings of the palate to our relations with the world?
We travel non-stop, in the interval between
The lifting of one cooking lid and another, going after
The taste of fermented soya beans
Stopping by a pool of dried soy sauce
Studying the traces

In my old home, shabby but comfortable, I remember
Those plump eggplants mother bought
Placed right in the centre of the sitting room, like Buddha
To be revered. In time life turned chaotic, abroad, alone
I could never recapture that taste in my cooking

With what mixed feelings, I wonder, your parents
Had followed the flux of emigrants and crossed the wide seas
Their vocabulary becoming infiltrated with hybrid fruit, new vegetables
Their tongues slowly getting used to foreign seasonings
Like many of their generation, everyone began to drift away

From a centre, their appearance changed. But now and then
From shreds of something here and bits of
Something else there we discover a vaguely familiar taste
Like meat and skin cooked to a mush, gone apart
Back together again: that taste of ourselves, extinct, distinct

Sushi for two

I want to be the seaweed that rolls you up.
Will you wrap yourself round my clumsy body?

Can you stand those bright sea urchin eggs on me?
Loving you I have to love them too—octopus, cucumber, crab fillet and all.

Countless rice rolls of the past return to haunt us.
Plain tea or saké? Feels like the choice before a thousand crossroads.

Reaching for you where you are soft and chewy I hit the hidden spikes.
Claws of the soft-shelled crab—like spider legs—playing for love?

Shedding layers of clothes you stop as if shuddering.
Nearing the coiled core is like touching some pain deeply buried.

With no idea of how I taste my rawness drives you away.
Your natural pungency, hot and mustardy, hurts me too.

We fall silent, laid out side by side on the dish, like strangers.
A word or two perhaps but my stomach feels queasy with old grudges.

When love is no more evening meals are mere consumption of matter.
When home is no more maybe only the soul of clams will give shelter?

From different cities we came, with different winters behind us.
We enjoy each other's bright hues but what keeps up apart?

I chew slowly, digesting your deep sea fibre.
You go still in the noise as I melt on you tongue.

Monster City

Alice drove down the road
Lined with bodies changing into monsters,
Wove her way through the city, provoking a roar
From its concrete entrails,
A drug called joy
Spread through the underground network from needle to needle,
Colonizing the human economy,
Alice heard various rumours from inside the car;
A seven-foot spider woman walking on the midnight streets,
Under the flyovers street-sleepers quietly vaporizing.
The monsters chose this historic moment
To come and join the masquerade.
(Power accumulated below ground
Will erupt at any time.)
Alice heard a sad voice crying:
Yes, my Miss Fantasm, we did once love one another,
But I have to kill you now!
The emotion in the voice made her tremble;
Tumours had suddenly begun to surface above ground in waves,
A virus was proliferating from harbour to peak.
Hard to know if the creepy-crawlies were men or beasts;
Every towering building stood in great peril.
Alice seemed to recall she had another identity.
But why was she embroiled in this misty legend?
Escaping at breakneck speed
From this city in facial metamorphosis,
It was so easy to crash into the zone of darkness.
The beasts were working on her—
They thought her the sole surviving human.
As she made a turn in the broad daylight street,
Humans fired at her, said she was a monster with a human mask.
The winding lanes were a maze with no way out.
Passersby might at any time change,
Grow viper-heads.

Alice didn't know why she was involved in this battle,
Didn't know whether her pursuers were her lovers
Or enemies.
Was that some strange beast up ahead
Or a boa?
She pulled out her gun and strafed the emptiness.
In the rear-view mirror she saw her own face
Among the killers in pursuit;
She accelerated at full throttle
To escape from her own city.

China Doll

In the look you give me
I see many mysterious 'she's

You seem to be looking at a see-through floral chiffon gown?
You ask me whether I have a crimson bra on underneath

You say you like high-slit silver brocade *cheongsams* with a pattern of
tiny blue flowers
You are curious to find me not wearing a torn floral fabric, with bare
shoulders

Sorry, now very few people are carried off as concubines by brigands
Sorry, on the street where I live, there are no big red lanterns hanging
high

Hey, I'm not a China doll with flowers in my hair
Hey, I'm very sorry that I can't make up for your time-warp

Perhaps now she's wearing a pair of Gucci shoes to chase a shadow
Bumpy Pottinger Street mocks her stiletto heels

You feel sorry not to find Chinese-style lapels in my wardrobe:
By the side of the statue of Buddha willows are brushing the fishes'
world.

Hey, it's a pity pollution has become so serious, the river bed is all
silted up
Hey, even the land is being speculated on and becoming valuable now

Perhaps now she's wearing an Anne Klein suit, like the main character
In a Hollywood movie, and speaking at some important financial
conference.

She's got relatives who've migrated to Australia, and often she spends her
holidays in America and Canada;
She's got a shawl with a pattern of plum blossoms, and likes
cheongsams covered with gold embroidery.

She reads foreign fashion magazines with care, and follows Western
taste
Her look reproaches me for continuing to distinguish the Oriental body

From the look she gives me
I see many mysterious 'you's

Lien Chao

LIEN CHAO, born in 1950, came to Canada in 1984 to pursue her postgraduate studies. Her Ph.D. thesis, *Beyond Silence: Chinese Canadian Literature in English*, published in 1997 by TSAR Publications, won the 1997 Gabrielle Roy Award for Criticism. She is currently working on a bilingual (English/Chinese) long narrative poem and a creative non-fiction. Living in Toronto with her parents and spouse, she teaches people with special needs.

Political Ice Age

What?

"Dragon gives birth to dragon.
Phoenix breeds more phoenixes.
Descendants of rats
know only how to dig holes."

What?

"Rats should be drowned.
Rats cannot mix with dragons.
Rats are rats.
Rats cannot become dragons."

What?

"This is the law of blood.
Of how species reproduce themselves.
And the law of blood
will never change."

What kind of logic is this?
Where does this edict come from?

Thousands of us
teenagers
puzzled by this zoo talk
opening our innocent eyes wide
raising questions

Who are the dragons?
Who are the rats?

confusion confusion confusion

What?

"Those born in the families of workers,
poor peasants, lower-middle peasants,
revolutionary cadres, and revolutionary soldiers

belong to the Five Red Categories,
and belong to the dragon class.
Born red, they will remain red
generation after generation
forever and ever red
dragon giving birth to dragons."

"Descendants of dragons
you are the steering force of the revolution."

What?
"Those born in the families of landlords,
rich peasants, reactionaries,
social dregs, and Rightists
belong to the Five Black Categories
belong to the rat class.

Born black, they will remain black
generation after generation
forever and ever black
rats giving birth to rats."

"Descendants of rats
you are the targets of the revolution."

What kind of logic is this?
Whose policy is this?

foredoom foredoom foredoom

A Tide of Madness

It had never been so crowded before
squeezed among a dozen people
on the bare floor
between two rows of seats
in a forest of human legs
my knees touching my chest
like an unborn baby
curved inside my mother's womb

Pitch dark
not a single star
the train moving
swiftly, on shiny rails
overloaded
all the cars
passengers
crowded
like knotted pines
human limbs entwined
no water
no food
couldn't move
couldn't sleep
sweat
body odour
in the moving car

To Beijing!
A human tide of madness
like a tornado
sweeping over the country
in an era of turmoil

Serve the People

Days and weeks passed
as the green creek flew by the village
the neck of an hourglass
slowly, slowly
two years went by

One day
twilight
a notice arrived
from the Party committee:
I am officially transferred
recruited to work on the railroad

Farewell
   wild date trees on the hillside
   golden rice fields outside the village
   green vegetable patches behind the houses
   silver cotton plants in the fields

Farewell
   the freezing yellow earth
   dark-skinned children
   wrinkle-faced peasants
   and the reservoir built with our bare hands

Confinement
on clanking iron wheels
embarking on a moving cage
the career of a railway steward

With a dozen young women
all about twenty years old
short hair
strong and vigorous

in navy-blue uniforms

In front of the train
we lined up
like shiny nails on the rails
like soldiers, we obeyed
order and discipline

Serve the people, our motto:
        opening the door, closing the door
        helping the old, caring for the sick
        moving luggage, washing the floor
        serving hot water, cleaning the toilets
        solving problems, delivering babies
        and organizing political studies

inside the moving train:
        fluorescent lights flooded down
        from the ceilings, pale and blue
        on rows of hard seats
        drowsy passengers nodding off

outside
        stormy sky, pitch dark
        lightning the ruling king
        the train shaking, wheels clanking
        locomotive puffing, charging ahead

From the loudspeakers a scratchy voice
waking up the passengers:
"Dear revolutionary passengers,
it's time for political study
Let's recite the *Quotations* together."
"Be determined, be not afraid to die . . . "
"Criticize individualism and revisionism."
"U.S. imperialism is a paper tiger."

An inspector
from the Railway Bureau
arrived at my car
stood at the entrance

> Looking around
> I felt pride:
> my car, clean and tidy
> my service, impeccable

Mr. Inspector
a white glove on his left hand
touching here, feeling there
along the windows
in the space between luggage racks
underneath the tables
behind the doors
touching here, feeling there
raising his gloved hand
flicking his fingers
examining the snow-white glove
Mr. Inspector, twitching
his smallpox-scarred face
narrowing his eyes
uttering a judgement:
"You should put politics ahead of your work!"

> My silence
> my answer

Mr. Inspector, frowning
spit, changed his subject
"I heard you want to be an on-train announcer, is that so?
So you dislike your current steward's job, is that so?
You don't want to serve the people, is that so?"

Mr. Inspector
hysterical, shouting
"An on-train radio announcer is the Party's tongue,
the job is not for someone like you,
a bourgeois flower,
from a bourgeois intellectual's family,
having an uncle in Taiwan.
You are politically untrustworthy
you want to be an announcer
you must be day-dreaming!
Day-ay-dreaming!"

I stood
as if at a market square
as if at the stake
from the nozzle of the hot water kettle
steam puffing out
scorching my fingers
blurring my vision
burning me
branding me
in front of the passengers

> I am a railway steward
> like everyone else?
> Why am I still
> an unwanted person?
> an old wound reopened
> heredity, genealogy
> unburied ghosts
> haunted me

As stewards
we lived our youth on rails
on moving vehicles
no beginning, no end
moving tirelessly on the two tracks

until completely drained
we developed arthritis, stomach ulcers
incurable insomnia

By then, we were worn-out old stewards
meteors shooting across the sky at night
rusty nails being pulled out from the rails
one by one, gradually and silently
replaced by a new generation
of younger stewards in their twenties
short hair, healthy, energetic, in sparkling new uniforms
as we did the old stewards today

And we, to be retired from the train
to work behind the railway station
in poorly lit laundry rooms
in a food-packing factory
in a warehouse of waste materials
no need to memorize train schedules anymore
just listen to the clanking wheels passing by
reminisce about the past
and busy our minds with lonesome memories

Gaik Cheng Khoo

GAIK CHENG KHOO, born in the year men landed on the moon, was raised in Malaysia. She lived in Singapore for a year and a half, did her B.A. in Austin, Texas from 1990-1993 and is now pursuing her Ph.D. in Interdisciplinary Studies at the University of British Columbia on gender and modernity in Malaysian literature and film. She is interested in Cultural Studies, Women's Studies, cinema, and post-colonial literature and theory. She has lived in Vancouver since 1993 and writes mostly short fiction. Her work has been published in the *Toronto South Asian Review* and *West Coast Line.*

Memories of food/people

Mother

is dim sum

waking up at six a.m. with whispers of "wansee-wansee"
a babyish term we children never outgrew
for desires, impossible to articulate in grown-up tongue
a secret code and bond only between Mother and us

Pa turns over to his side
snores unimpressed under hills of pillows
the morning newspaper she brought in folded on the bed
will keep him occupied when he wakes
to his cup of Milo and boiled egg

We set out before school in her modest little car
before Grandmother passed away
we were a string of females
three generations long
who streamed into busy Halomon
past the golden carp in the pond making watery lickety sounds
in our expandable school uniforms
excited and made hungry by the wafting smells
of *harkow, siew mai, char siew pow*
        "And fishball, don't forget fishball!" my elder sister reminded

Now Halomon no longer stands
now neither sisters nor I have to guide Ah Ma
over the bridge across the pond
impatient with her
overanxious to eat and run
not wanting to be late for school

"Your father, he doesn't even know what my favourite food is.
Ask him, ask him and he can only guess,"
my mother, married for over thirty years
shakes her head
resigned to Pa's contentment
the hills of pillows rising and falling

Father

is Indian mee
at Bangkok Lane
Saturday noon
post-girl guide meeting

"*Mi goreng, tak mau sotong, tak mau telur,
taugeh chay chay,*" he'd tell the frying brother
if the eldest, he wouldn't have a thing to say
the sarong-clad man already accustomed to Pa's weekly order
if I ordered with squid and egg
Pa's eyes would bulge when the bill arrived
"I forgot, sorry." In truth no amount of guilt stained me
Mother's generosity immuned us
even as he grumbled away about food prices and we moved
through the rising lunchtime heat wave
to the ice *kacang* stand for refreshing coconut water
and maybe, if I were persuasive
ais kacang bungkus for the family's afternoon tea

In front of her bedroom mirror
parading one office outfit after another
for us girls to compare, inviting comments
worried about the skirts hugging her hips too well
Mother suddenly chuckled

"Perhaps it's a good thing your father's stingy with food.
Imagine how fat we'd all become if he were generous!"

Auntie Bessie

is homemade fastfood

Fried rice with leftovers
very simple, tastier than Mother's, or
vermicelli fried with beansprouts with hand-plucked ends
laced with a can from China I have failed to find in Vancouver
combing through shelf after dusty shelf in Chinatown
not pig's trotters, but some brown porky dish with soft chewable bones
floating in flavoured grease and soya sauce
it made the *bee hoon* slide unstuck in the wok

This, she boasted, was prepared for under five dollars
to feed two teenage children and an office-weary husband
we helped ourselves to more
she smiled, pleased. In later years, Mother wrote
telling of how Aunt Bessie secretly replaced our pretty mugs
gifts from an uncle in Montreal
with the free-gift glasses she got from buying Ovaltine
I suppose she thought the Canadian mugs matched her kitchen fittings
better than they did our crazy eclectic family
she always did have an eye for attractive things in our house

Sometimes passing Broadway on the bus
I catch certain aromas of cooking that is her
I don't go in, convinced it won't taste the same
and at three times the price, it just isn't fair

Pama

is handmade pineapple tarts and scones
learnt from a former Eurasian employer
something we had never seen or tasted before
only read about in Enid Blyton books

She is

fish curry with little brown mustard seeds where
sometimes lady's fingers swim among other curried edibles
and bought Indian sweet treats from Thaipusam:
sugar-coated peanuts, deep-fried unnameable goodies
crunchy, twisted, spiced with caraway seed
I see them set out in rows at the All-India Restaurant at Main and 49th
like Deepavali open-house visits where
children, shedding their initial shyness
play and sweat in their colourful best in the garden
the men indulge in beef *rendang* and politics
the women compliment the hostess' recipes
and Pama, in good spirits after returning from her days off
seems rejuvenated by her sari's brightness
fresh jasmine in her coiled hair
nose-ring in place
I miss her

Me

i'm greedy for gravy
Mother's weekly email about so-and-so's divorce
cousins having babies, relatives being robbed
the usual dose of adultery and family squabbles
real-life soap operas interspersed with recipes
like *sambal heh bee* or
nonya brinjal masak lemak,
"Add more thick *santan* for extra gravy," she writes
knowing me only too well
"and don't forget to squeeze in more tamarind juice.
Finally, sprinkle on a lavish amount of fried shallots."
Mother's answer to every garnish translates into extra "leow" on my terms
more gravy or sauce or simply untranslatably
more

Peng

"What I miss most about being in Hong Kong?"
during Grandma's funeral he mused
"Malaysian savouries, not the desserts."
At fifteen, living at home at still loving Nonya cakes
I couldn't agree, couldn't understand
but cousin, now I do, from the farthest recesses of my olfactory glands
and the deepest yet brightest spark of nostalgia
Penang char koay teow and *sar hor fun* call out to me
I long to sit, sweating in a *kopi-tiam* drinking *kopi peng* with old men
lives full and long, boasting of their offspring's achievements
oh give me
that simple plastic wrapped eighty-cent rice roll
unrolled and roughly cut
doused with hoisin, chili, soya sauce
and *heh ko,* diluted just right
sprinkled with sesame and fried shallots

To us, Peng, myself, other cousins
beckon Sydney, Vancouver, and L.A.
Malaysian cuisine aplenty
but this appetite satiated, will our longing
for the people and home we miss
be curbed as well?
hard to say whether food or family comes first

Unsure
I stand by and take notes
observe the rituals of my loved ones
far and near
their favourite dishes, sauces
listen to their stomachs agree or disagree with my cooking
"There's something missing," my sister likes to insist about my fried rice
but gingerly, not wanting to bruise my ego *cuisineaste*
we know there's no substitute for Auntie Bessie's

Vancouver seems a far stretch from Penang
yet surprisingly, my lover
a child in him somewhere, also recalls
longtime snacks of sour plums
peeling haw flakes from their pink and green paper rolls
sticky raisins in tiny green del monte boxes
as if a multi-flavoured bridge spans across the Pacific
drawing our separate cultural childhoods closer together
and all those years of anonymity between two young strangers
disappear as we merge into the Big Blue Marble

Mi goreng, tak mau sotong, tak mau telur, taugeh chay chay: fried yellow noodles, no squid, no egg, lots of bean sprouts

Sambal heh bee: spicy dried shrimp.

Nonya brinjal masak lemak: eggplant cooked with coconut milk (*santan*).

Heh ko: a sticky, smelly prawn paste.

Big Blue Marble: a children's television program that aired in Malaysia.

Thuong Vuong-Riddick

THUONG VUONG-RIDDICK (pronounced Tyoong Vyong) was born of Chinese descent in Hanoi in 1940. She moved with her family at age fourteen to Saigon where she completed a B.A. in French Literature. During the Vietnam War in 1962, she went to Paris to earn a B.A. in Philosophy and an M.A. and Ph.D. in French Literature at Sorbonne. She emigrated to Montreal seven years later. Vuong-Riddick is the author of *Two Shores/Deux Rives*, published by Ronsdale Press, and her work has been anthologized in the U.S. and taught in American universities, including Yale. She has given readings, lectures, and workshops all over Canada and the U.S., and currently resides in Delta, B.C.

Searching

I belong to a country that I have left.
                              —Colette

I belong to a country that I have left.
A country of small streets and villages
where people know their neighbours
from birth to old age.

I belong to a country where
the seasons bring few changes
between winter and summer no difference
except for the rains, when it rains.

I belong to a country
you cannot look for
on maps, in books, movies.
Even I hardly recognize it from the pictures
I saw yesterday in a calendar.

I belong to a country of the mind
with friends and relatives
scattered in Canada, America, France, Australia,
Vietnam.

J'appartiens
á un pays
que j'ai quitté.

Thoung thuôc vê, Thoung thuôc vê . . .

My Beloved Is Dead in Vietnam

for Trinh Cong Son, author of The Mad Woman

Dark or blue, all beloved, all beautiful.
Numberless eyes have seen the day.
They sleep in the grave,
and the sun still rises.

              —Sully Prudhomme

My beloved is
Dead in Diên Biên Phu
Dead in Lao Kay, dead in Cao Bang
Dead in Langson, dead in Mong Cai
Dead in Thai Nguyên, dead in Hanoï
Dead in Haïphong, dead in Phat Diêm
Dead in Ninh-Binh, dead in Thanh Hoa
Dead in Vinh, dead in Hatinh
Dead in Hue, dead in Danang, dead in Quang Tri
Dead in Quang Ngai, dead in Qui Nhon
Dead in Kontum, dead in Pleiku
Dead in Dalat, dead in Nha-Tranh
Dead in My Tho, dead in Tuy Hoa
Dead in Biên-Hoa, dead in Ban Me Thout
Dead in Tayninh, dead in Anloc
Dead in Saigon, dead in Biên Hoa
Dead in Can Tho, dead in Soc Trang

Vietnam, how many times
I have wanted to call your name
I have forgotten
the human sound.

The Whirlwind of History

During *May 1968* I lived in Paris,
my sister, brother and I, we were students.
We knew those burning days of May:
Paris, covered with barricades,
policemen attacking
students throwing stones.
Tear-gas everywhere
in the Latin Quarter.
"Zut! Encore des flics!"
Surprised tourists ran with students
hunted by police.

My sister Hoa landing from Vietnam
felt quite at home,
stocked rice in the cupboard.
Smoke and screams where
the quotidian scene.
Speeches inflamed the nation.
Revolution was spreading to the Western world,
but no one was killed, except by accident.

As May was fading,
startling news arrived from Saïgon:
My mother, brother and sisters would join us.
They had lived through the *New Year offensive,
the famous Têt 1968.*
"One hundred rockets a day
during one hundred days"
as the Vietcong claimed.

Then Montpellier in the south,
but even here the children faced
the French police:

no resident visa.
I needed a country
where we all could live,
Canada.

In Montréal I found two jobs,
But history followed me,
when *La Crise d'Octobre 1970* exploded,
students told me:
"The most tragic episode of our history!"
I thought: "Only one killed!"

One by one they arrived:
five years in all
to overcome
distance, administrative papers.
It was finished,
January 1975.

Saïgon fell in April,
my father died in December.

Blues

Coming from the tropics,
the hardest for me in the Paris winter:
not to live
in the daylight.

Days so short
they could not be appreciated.

This panic:
my life being engulfed
in an endless tunnel of the night.

I never imagined
Paris as a grey old woman,
the endless avenues,
metro travel,
the boredom of Sorbonne classes,
loud university restaurants,
endless forms for a single book.

I browse in the bookstores,
meet friends in the coffee shops.
We speak of Jean-Luc Godard,
Eisenstein, Bergman, Antonioni.

Outside of Vietnam,
Paris, largest Vietnamese city
in the world,
clans formed again

I began to read about the war,
weary of separating the world
into bad and good
knowing that

every moment
someone fell beneath
a burst of gunfire.

Both sides using the same methods
to justify the slaughter
of a population
they claim to protect
or wish
to set free.

Three generations were sacrificed
so many mowed down
in the prime of life.

But no one today
can see our wounds.

Use an x-ray
to photograph our souls—
you will glimpse
a landscape
incomprehensible
even to ourselves.

Spiders Are People Too . . .

On this side of Paradise
"Spiders are people too," I am told.
You should see
the good people of Victoria
along the ocean with their dogs
strolling, racing,
unaware of the Chinese walkers,
joking in Cantonese.

You should see the fat ducks,
wild geese of all kinds,
swimming at their leisure
in ponds, in lakes, in bays,
with so many friends and admirers,
always ready to feed them
as soon as they appear.

In newspapers you can see photographs
of cats, dogs, and pets of all sorts.
They have a society for animal rights,
grooming salons, even cemeteries.

I remember our world
where people are not even spiders.

Across the Country

My beloved rose early in the morning,
started the motor in darkness,
devoured towns and cities
on roads full of traffic.
He rolled down the valleys,
climbed plateaus
where the water is blue and clear.
He chose mountainous roads.
All day long
nothing frightened him.

Because he was born in a free country
space belonged to him.

He Covered Me With a Blanket

He covered me
when I was sick,
useless, hopeless,

when I was naked
in the world's eyes.

In Montpellier station,
he took all my luggage
on his back,
put his arms around me.
Mother said:
He is the one for you.

When my family arrived from France,
Ma, Na, Mi, Kieng, Tchieng, Te, Ti,
he covered them all
with his signature.

It was like
the warm blanket
I felt around my father
who never touched me
his whole life, as I recall.
(He was too Confucian—
Man shouldn't touch woman unless they are married.)

It was like
the invisible shawl
knitted by nun's prayers
in the convent at Dalat
to protect me
from life's perils.

It was like
the network of women in Quebec—
Monique, Martine, Jeanne, Gloria, Marie-Louise—
who rescued me;
And Marie-Claire, Mary, Gloria, Chantal, Monique
who sponsored my cousin's family,
so that through the long winter
I felt *notre amitié*
as a warm current
under the icy cold.

It was like
the people on the streets of Victoria—
bus drivers, friends from Aikikai,
Jean-Louis, Diane, Cor, Yoke, Dave,
Lloyd, Andrée, Chie, Fong—
who made us their family.

It was like
an immense quilt,
of all the help and love
I received over
years and oceans.

It is this human warmth
of the country
I belong to.

Glenn Deer

GLENN DEER, of Chinese and German descent, was born in Edmonton in 1959. A graduate of the University of Alberta and York, he currently teaches Canadian Literature, Asian Canadian/American writing, and rhetorical theory in the English Department at the University of British Columbia. He is the author of a collection of poetry, *Excuses for Archery* (Longspoon, 1982), and a critical study, *Postmodern Canadian Fiction and the Rhetoric of Authority* (McGill-Queen's, 1994).

The Eurasian Album

for Fred, Jim, and Ramona

I

Photographs of the great walled countries that divide us:
your trip to Beijing, our walks through Berlin
mapping the racial geography
of our parents' refugee pasts, and missing
from these albums
airline tickets to imaginary Eurasian
homelands.

In 1972, riffs of "A Whiter Shade of Pale."
What decadent music could these Eurasian kids smuggle
to the communist East? We wanted to import the drama
of paleness with our visas, for the border guards
at Checkpoint Charlie would miss the irony,
and Procol Harum could skip the light fandango through the Wall,
a gift for an expectant cousin, an official party musician.

Clutching our rock albums, under layers of clothes,
we learn to look at the border guards, look at them
straight in the eyes: we have nothing
to declare.

Our cousin hurtles down the autobahn in his yellow Beetle,
a "Big Apple" sticker on the side. After ten varieties of beer,
he sings for the women on the street corners: Alexanderplatz in '72,
a West Berliner and two German-Chinese teenagers in bell bottoms
and shag hair, later we stick out in the grey flannel
concrete housing projects of East Berlin where we cool our drinks
in a bathtub of ice: Germans here want our clothes but despise our
looks.

Don't walk so close to the barbed wire fence, warns my aunt.
I don't care if they shoot me, says my defiant sister. I'm a
Canadian. You should dress like a German, thinks my aunt.

I think, we should dress like Red Guards.
I wonder, is the fence electrified?

Several men in Alexanderplatz ask if my sister is for sale,
her Asian eyes, makeup, black hair, Levis compel capitalistic
bidding in the public squares of bland East German conformity:
the hailing of the Other eastern body. She walks closer to my uncles,
gripping their broad shoulders, pushing through the street of men.

This is what repression builds.

I am riding a bicycle through windy fields of rye,
through the rural village of Mahlow, face and hair
conspicuous, suspicious as I wheel past the barracks
of the Russian troops, composing possible Canadian
excuses they will not understand

as I smash into a small boy
running into my path from the shadows of the fields:

I say "Dear boy, dear boy" as he weeps.
He stares at me astonished, looking into the face
of a Mongol rider.

My cousin plays the Beatles's "White Album" and composes songs
for solidarity: he is flying to Moscow to conduct folkloric opera
for the oppressed.

White Russian mythologies.

Under the communist regime we wear boots of felt,
museum footware in Potsdam, Sans Souci, the common people
polishing the gleaming palace floor of Frederick the Great,

the endless shuffling of tourists and Berliners,
corridors of class bereavements.

In the great mirrored halls, turn to face the other.
You have the face of an Asian, but your mother is German:
and why did you marry a Chinaman, she is once asked by a
Ukrainian woman, a former friend: now I think of the eastern horde
swelling in her imagination, now black, now blonde.

II

They go over the barbed wire or smuggle packages through the wall:
they buy boat passages from Hong Kong and Bremen. Weeks of
rolling water and heaving stomachs. My parents' middle-passage,
their Eurasian journeys replayed without ending, now a son unpacks
a suitcase full of histories.

So I always ask why you left, why you chose him, why you took
on the labour of transformation, this experiment in hybridity?

   fourteen of your best reasons for leaving:

You were trying to replace your anger with a country.

Your suitcases were packed at the age of twelve, ready to jump the
train, escape the bombing.

You were looking for the underworld spirit of your dead mother in
a border zone, world on the edge:
you chose Lloydminster, half in Alberta,
half Saskatchewan.

You wanted to live in a border town where Chinese, German,
Ukrainian, Polish, and Czech were spoken, where you could escape
from language to language.

You wanted to buy two full bags of groceries, neither of them
containing green potatoes.

You were seduced by the lure of colonization, to settle a new world
unpitted by bombs, where your roof would never convulse in a shower
of shrapnel and splinters, sirens wailing in the air raid nocturne
where subway shelters left no scent of the friends who disappeared
in the hail of fire.

You heard the invitation of my father's voice, embraced the man
from Hoi Ping, turned against the face of Aryan control, embraced
the man.

You needed the job in the Lloydminster Hotel.

Your body crawled with the Berlin voices of betrayal, the pain of
occupation, ideological truces: friends resented Americans,
you dreamed of Canada.

You had a German boyfriend who wanted to sail to Canada: he was a good
dancer and promised to help you find work.

You needed to leave the dancer, full of himself and cheap talk,
it was your first lesson in male weakness.

But you looked up at the cook, leaving for work, rolling a cigarette,
offering you a ride home, dessert at the diner, voice of kindness:
the glow of the radio.

You liked the tilt of his fedora, the cut of his overcoat, his brown
eyes.

You poured a pan full of bread crumbs over him in the restaurant
kitchen, revenge for putting that dead mouse in your apron pocket:

Later, you held his hand and walked from Saskatchewan
to Alberta in the snow. You could never leave him.

Andy Quan

ANDY QUAN is third generation Chinese-Canadian and fifth generation Chinese-American. He was born in Vancouver, B.C. in 1969. He has studied at Pearson College, Trent University, and York University. Outside of Canada, he has lived in Denmark, Ecuador, Spain, Belgium, and the United Kingdom, and has worked for the International Lesbian and Gay Association in Brussels, and a gay men's HIV prevention organization in London. His poetry and short fiction have been published in various literary journals and in six anthologies of gay fiction. He is also a singer-songwriter and is presently living in Sydney, Australia.

En route

Mother's great-grandparents
arrived on Hawaiian shores
to live and plant rice

Father's grandparents
sold an empire of shoes
and sent a son to gold mountain

Father's sister lifted out
of Grandfather's produce store
became a stewardess

Mother arrived in Canada
with no winter clothes
to be wed to my father

I come from a long line
of travellers
so it should not surprise me
to lay down roots and leave
veins from my heart
branching out to
the ends of my fingertips

I hurl out to the stratosphere
floating while
the stewardess brings drinks
for my throat sore
from parting words

like a flock of geese
I follow blindly
to a destination
written deeply under folds
of skin, blood, tissue

words on bone though
my false heart
above the clouds
says this cannot be me again
leaving all I have made

Via Puerto Quito, km. 89

in the outhouse: immobilized
forehead jewelled with sweat
sudden fear rolling forward
a tarantula lounging on
the wooden door which I push
open as far as I can reach

I emerge bent like grass
to a full-bellied night sky
crescent-moon fallen down
into a cheshire cat's grin
bouquets of yellow stars
on the opposite horizon
tensed to be flung onstage

This is romance:
a created mythology
minor pain, redemption
though these words are not
the clean flowing water
needed here
fall away easily
like heat under wet seasons

Señora Gordillo
inquires if I am well

That night I dream
of wrinkled angels
labouring in tropical heat
my first world guilt
elevates them into flight

I shield my eyes so as
to not look up their skirts

still I notice that while
my insides are dry and empty
theirs are like cactus hearts

Los Bancos, Ecuador

The Old Women of Seville

The old women draped in polyester flowers
as bright as language

they are slabs of cured meat swaying
under gravity's trance but immoveable

their mouths fountains
bosoms a just made bed rumpled by children

lined faces intricate as marble inlays
on floors of cathedrals built upon faraway riches

they are gritty as street beggars, a pickpocket
a man sleeping in hot night air on the bodega's sidewalk

and graceful as the gesture of a queen
surrendering her jewels to change the world

stubborn, too, as the man who received them
lauded, condemned, false father of newness, of genocide

these old duchesses say ¡beautiful! with tear-stained eyes
generations follow suit

heat rising
like a second coming
fans that suddenly appear like a scattering of leaves
the sound of a million doves
                                        settling

                                                    Seville, Spain

Belonging

People follow love to this continent and decide to stay
long after romance has shrivelled like a seed without soil
they open bookshops, teach English, write poetry, and marry
cover their roots with each snowfall and
hide unease in the vowels of a new language
content to join novelty to an old tapestry
like the restoration of a masterpiece
or the slow shifting of continents
something familiar with a scent of change

People tell me this isn't quite the right time to travel in Europe
and true, the night comes quickly like melancholy
the statues in great Sans Souci were boarded up like outhouses

but winter trees have their own beauty
the greys in cold seasons have many shades
people at times are unguarded
like those that have just woken
and with tourists few
cities become like the ends of parties
where those who stay are those who belong

Berlin, Germany

First sun

The first sun after winter travels, I take in
light like a pop star preening on a balcony
that juts out like a proud chin. Human buoys
bob four flights below, young men on mopeds
through cement waves imagining themselves
speedboats cutting through the city's harbour

A book of Yeats and the sun warm my face spread
outwards like a drop of ink on silk or messages
relayed of the identity of two lovers seen
entering arched doorways in a narrow street
a clock in a turreted tower chimes as they kiss

If I dropped this book of poetry its spine would break
like Roman columns, pages scattering through walkways
swaths of white like a summer flock of sailboats
dotting the ocean, flags of surrender
capitulating to a piracy where the past is stolen
and hoarded into this first bright day

One carefree motion and the words of an Irishman
sweep through Italian streets, pieces of clouds cut free

Savona, Italy

First night

the streetlamps flood through curtains
constant traffic voices sing
into crisp night air engines idling
distant horns are memories
that will not leave. Each time
the door opens to the drag bar
a blast of music escapes as if
thinking of too many things
at once and you lose one

are the cars noisier here because
sounds echo in narrow streets
squeal of brakes bounce off of
balconies, windows? is it
a sensitive hour half past three?
laughter, motorcycle transmission
the groaning of passing autos
ricocheting louder out of the
narrow wedge between clock hands

I try to shut off my senses
one by one but I will not sleep tonight
percussion of high heels on pavement
orchestra of dawn traffic, alto hoots
and baritone howls. insistent melodies

Brussels, Belgium

Passport problems

Certain Scandinavians bow and speak Japanese to
me although I am not Japanese

Travelling in Europe if treated as a foreigner I
simply switched countries, but this time I have
come to stay and tire of these strange curiosities and
disdain

I crave their pigments to darken, for a sudden
blooming of Asian eyes, to soften their high curved
cheekbones, their European angles

Christmas holidays they stop me at the border and
examine my passport with ultraviolet rays:

"There are many forged passports lately, Canadian
passports, many Asians, using forged Canadian
passports"

"There are Asians living in Canada" The border
guard replies defensively "I know"

On this continent, he knows my destiny better than
I, to be stopped at their imaginary borders, my
black hair and slant eyes shouting at them brighter
than any flag they have ever seen

Stockholm, Sweden

Monday Night Entertainment

like the idea of a word before it is formed
something on the dusk blue horizon
the hushed expectancy of the gathered crowd
fifty pairs of eyes all straining out to the distance

there, the pointed star, a pinprick
doubles into eyes, a widening god
of knowledge and mystery

a great winged form the eyes
joined by a face and body riding
the tropic wind the pink afterglow
of day disappearing the ocean's
quickening breath fills
the clothes of spectators
startled and giddy in their new forms

the unthinking boeing thunders
down upon the seawall
swoops over their heads flashing
a sleek shining belly

people disperse slowly but slower
the ones who wished just
one moment they'd lost
their consciousness
in a roar of engines
an occasion of white light

Raratonga, Cook Islands

names of fuschias

I gave up the habit the same day walking
through Schönbrunn park I read the names of fuschias
as passers-by tasted summer through cloth and skin
    corallina   *gitana*   *display*
    It was like noticing after a time a cut has healed
    the sun has shifted or your fingernails   *lady*
need cutting again   *thumb*
  earl of beaconsfield   children in carriages
      sleigh bells   pushed by mothers
          a roller-blader skating backwards.

On a work trip to Vienna already I'd decided
to change capitals, Brussels to London, leave my first job,
   live in my own language again. Christian's voice
baby   over my shoulder. "I never know
  blue eyes   the names of flowers
red shadows, igloo maid   Why do they look so sad?"

                       I disagree.
True, the buds hang downwards but
      it is a layered joy multiplying, the petals
temptation   a four-pointed star bending backwards
    the delicate whorled cup nestled perfectly
red   loin to loin the gangly stamens
buttons   reaching out to kick their legs in the air
    deutsche   *perle*

He explains that Vienna is surrounded   *flying*
          by forests which filter the air sweeping   *cloud*
                    into the city clean, new, the pungence
          clair de   of firs mixed with warm grass
          la lune   infusions of crimson and purple buds
                    A child's voice bubbling   *marinka*
                              up from the groundwater
                         —*you were to be something by this age*—
my stare   *golden*   fixes on flowers
magenta   *glow*   and white,
pink   *rose*   and mauve
checkerboard
          the pastoral Sunday sounds of leisure
                                                  nightingale
          are like and unlike any other orchestra

I think of how I move from city to city   *flash*
          maybe will never own a garden
                    like my mother's, the violet and orange
          fuschia I cannot now identify by name
     petals falling in the Austrian royal park and me
          giving up the habit of believing   *papagena*
                    that I'd know one day what I want to do,
jackshahan   that blooms of desire or choices in life are singular.

                                                  Vienna, Austria

Ritz Chow

RITZ CHOW arrived in Canada with her parents from Hong Kong on a blustery October night in 1972. She grew up in the Riverdale neighbourhood of Toronto. Her writing has appeared in *Contemporary Verse 2, Fireweed, Room of One's Own*, and various anthologies. Currently, she is exploring identity politics for women living with illness and disability for her M.A. in women's studies at Simon Fraser University. She has practiced as a pharmacist for seven years and lives in Vancouver.

a fall of grief

for christopher, surviving his lover's AIDS-*related death*

sitting on a misplaced log worn down with weather, i am smoothed by many moons rippling across the dark lake from the sky's selfless hold. a twisted tangle of roots hovers like a disfigured palm to my right, wrestling firelight and hair along my outstretched arms.

i have come to escape voices drifting in hollow human sounds beckoning leaves with forced laughter and campy hollers. i have come to feel the sleek remoteness of flat rocks. i have come to hear the tide shifting this lake's sifting floor, lifting stones one by one from their black echoing beds to the stark dryness of shore. i am here to undo a lake's million labours. in this quarter-light, my arms sizzle palely forward falling unseen towards the rattle at my feet. through my thin sneakers, the rocks offer up their circumscribed surfaces, edging off or sharply falling into themselves. the rocks gather slowly up, forming a quiet line for my warm hands. as i hold each one in moist palms, they whisper their solid dreams and hardened tears in a quick confession before i release them into air. as they fly, they whistle with home, spinning in that soft vortex between sound, before the splash of watery sheets wraps them in a wet embrace.

i sit contemplating the ineffectual state of my hands: giving nothing back to nothing, unable to change the lake by throwing back the shore. it's a matter of perimeters, how i think i am pushing back when each toss brings about a return i miss. boundaries shift, lean heavily one way or another, yet they remain.

this is how i fall into his grief as if into a plot. another handful of soil, another brilliant flower crackling with spectral intensity. i am running along a ragged shoreline, tossing it back in handfuls to haul them in—gaunt travellers of morphine waves, eclipsing toothy smiles and fuzzy blankets. in each breath, i hear an infant huddled into itself for a heartbeat, for a lungful of flaming air. in each death, i hear a crescendo: a modulation of adult-moan to child-gasp to watered foetal-screams. i am listening, here by the lake on a gutted log, ears fixed to the rattle of rocks on rocks, the hard noises of a lake pushing further from shore.

something chinese

it's a measure of arms, the way space occupies me as i lean one way then another, estimating the distance required to keep her from her self. i could take her in a quick absorption, replace each of her wild cells with rounds of moderation.

ten years ago, i used to be the wild one, running from the confines of skin, shaking fists and measuring the years with my scars. it is spring and her body has grown rampant, loosely fed by the dark globes of winter kitchens. the past mild winter has spared the thin roots of her hair—left it black still in the shimmering may light.

during dim sum, our eyes linger on the table, each of us waiting for a change in what we haven't said. "the *har kow* are plump today," she offers, and guides one to my bowl. this is what she knows of being a mother: silence around meals ringed by sudden offerings of food. my father sits and scans the other tables, waving now and then and leaving us to visit friends in the kitchen. i pour tea into her cup, hand poised with the shape of these chinese teapots: short plump faceless buddhas steaming with familiarity. how many times have we sat here, each of us eating into our own worlds mouthful by mouthful? each of us chewing with deliberation, tasting the time between us in the sticky rice. surrounded by leathery, gold-toothed faces, we signal for more tea.

once we are alone, my father says, "did she tell you about?" then he says something chinese and points to the right side of his chest. "cancer." the lump removed and found to be cancer. says, "all night, she cried." says, "call her when you have time."

i have come so far to escape her, fled with my body into the years. i have gathered all my possessions into boxes, labelled them and lifted them away. now she retrieves me without a word.

my breasts begin to hurt. i breathe and they twist, caught sparrows against my ribs. i want to get up and feel my breasts, touch them before they follow my mother in to her sleepless cells dividing without mercy in yellow globes of glands. my breasts are no longer young. no amount of exercise will keep them from their porous fat harbouring toxins and the final memories of my mother. everything she has fed me surfaces as dark blessings. what has she given me? what is her body doing to us all? i want to leave my breasts behind because of what they may become: my mother's daughters, after all.

family/life

over dinner once again
our eyes meet as mouths
to rice & oolong tea
& i want to say
ba'ba father
and show you my hands
what i am able to do
and what i won't
how i will never
give a bride's toast
at a chinese wedding banquet
like the ones you attend
in chinatown now
and again as children
of friends marry
how i will not buy
a house a store a car
how you must stop
realize i am everything
you've not heard of
from friends
from what immigrants
want for their children
in a new country

upon receipt of j's letter

you write this letter to me
and what do i do?
the legacy of your mother
etched in black, enjambing
line by line into this
cool spring afternoon.

what do we know
about our bodies anyway,
the way they move and swell
and pain us? there is life,
time on these sheets:
the house you grew up in smaller
than you have ever seen it;
your parents shrinking against
frames of wood; silence growing
despite all the words you toss
across tables, along halls; the deaths,
the births; the way you see them
struggle through bodies, thin-
lipped and voice-smooth. stark

against this shrinking
landscape, your roles
of daughter, of sister,
of mother-maybe, not-lesbian. you
with your packet of soup mix
and open novel in the kitchen,
holding the chair intently
down as if it would fly,
a magnet towards their grief.

what may i offer you?
each one of us grown
into disappointments. none
of us what our parents expected
yet we manage our lives,
write letters with care.

rambling

down in the slum time of the mind mingling with sorry people
who mumble and splutter into their hands a garden variety of hello i can't
and the sky is bleak with a blurred reminder of clouds and the sun is hot
so hot on the neck the spine melts and flesh liquefies and runs
along the long arm of a beautiful woman she so beautiful the sun so shy of
   her
and she asks me who i want in the innermost part of my charted heart
who of all the women i see in the long gone images of yester touches
kisses stretching in the absence of lips who do i want on whom do i runny
fingers along what breasts traceable in the mellow melt of night
brown skin white sheets the boundaries daring oblivion
bare brushed back the indentations of the straight spine down
to the half asked question of wet and soft and firm and supple
the palm and neck humid with sighs her voice a summer wind whistling
   between legs
arch and ache up the stern steering of come and go and i move i down in
   the drown
some new pond in the ragged wet throat of her command
the words watery greenly exploding light lean and sweet upon my tongue

three a.m.

we are full of small impossibilities
huddled to lamplight like moths
for direction, for the certainty of day
to guide us—thin insects buzzing
antennae, feeling for a way
into our own lives. we speak
to hear years spilling, rolling
flesh; the flat fears in eyes
weigh desires thin and we speak.
in your voice i hear a third heart,
a red stranger coming to form, pulling
our bodies to new angles, new
reservoirs of blood. i ask you to stay,
to mediate the progress of what i feel
to what i can't feel—this love
—not love affair tonight; how
we wish affection away, the tiny tears
in our perfect composure as we turn
flesh inward to sleep. you with your warmth
deep in the next room, somewhere breathing.

repetitions for a younger woman

thank you for the small. the inescapable objects holding vision intact
through cigarette smoke, through men swaggering beyond ears. Thank you
for the tiny, the minuscule blessings passing one surface to another,
object to skin to fibres behind eyes stringy with sense. thank you for
the something seconds, the ticking insistence of instances when you could
have stepped back or aside. thank you although i never make it easy,
uneasy with displays other than this smooth sleet of watching. thank you
for faded images demarcated in concentration and need. thank you for
objects of wood and stone, for warmth only shapes never dead may bestow.

it's a gift, isn't it? the minutes when one learns nothing and everything. the
seconds of recognizing someone the first and last time. the way time rides on
voices and clocks stop measuring, their hands and digital designs streaming
in a slip from tense. it's an hour backing into itself, passing so quickly it
swoops into its own departure.

thank you for stars that grow hard as diamonds in eyes when the looking is
done. thank you for the rasp and rattle of lungs gnawing air with crooked
teeth. thank you for colours, the wood of it all. a rare maple rippling
red beneath brown, carved with trails of sleep and insects. beyond the
window where i sit writing this, the night suspends black branches in
icy conversations, devouring completely their heat and bearing colours
down to transparency.

thank you for an evening, for the rub of life i measure against scales of
toronto disaster. thank you for the crisp wonder of other lives crackling
their flat intensities just beyond reach. thank you for 17ness surfacing
in circles around lips, those concentric years of who leading outward
until i imagine you thick-barked and ringed loose with seasons.

to bring you home

i press this page to bring you
through the rolling rails of night
your head weighed with passengers on an all-night bus
cursing american highways home to a monday
where i plan to meet you—arms serious as intent
where my body will betray every last emotion
our separation has managed to conceal
my skin old with stars, my flesh bursting to light
white heat of desire sifted by morning's frozen sun

you will alight from your journey, your veritable escape
baggage opening full of history—where you've been,
what you have touched and taken—folded
neatly in the seams of your mind
while i offer my hand, retrieve the days lost between us
in your fist the hours pressed tight into palms
so that neither of us may read
what the future suggests in its advance
everything so closed, even us

and i am writing to bring you back
to where my eyes meet your skin at the periphery
of freckles—brown mottled land tight with light
—beneath my fingers stretched for contact
for your touch across night i am
waiting with writing for another route
to your becoming back to me

Incantation

I will love you like wind,
intermittent and insistent,
unable to leave you
unmoved, hair or clothing.
I will race across your flesh
and leave no scar.
I will hover above you until
you scan the sky for me.
It's the search for the invisible
or the clues. You will know
    I am coming
when trees begin small trembles
at the tips of leaves,
when your scarf leaps
and dances towards the ocean.
There will be signs before I come.
I will arrive on your shoulder
from under a bird's wings,
hot from flight, burning with distance.

Pei Hsien Lim

PEI HSIEN LIM was born in Malaysia in 1953. He was an accomplished artist, dancer, choreographer, model, and later in life, an articulate spokesperson and champion for people living with AIDS. He was a founding member of Gay Asians of Toronto, helped organize Toronto's first Gay Street Patrol, and worked as a medical liaison for the Vancouver Persons With AIDS Society. He died in Vancouver in 1992. The poems included here are from a journal he kept in the last months of his life.

untitled one

In fetal curl
I lie still
Like a rock in a well

This too will pass
I know all about impermanence

Wordless pain changes
Into pain
More exact than words

Helpless sorrow wears a different outfit
For every occasion

So much lost
What little is left
Yet to be taken

untitled two

The other night
Tripping over the curb
Stumbling
I reached for the billboard
To steady myself

As I look up
My hand has landed on a poster
The Pacific Northwest Ballet
A dancer
In a perfect arabesque

I used to be able to do that

A brief fleeting instant
I remember joy

With broken tenderness
My right hand cradled left
I continued my journey home

untitled three

I love and hate
Cherry blossoms
So beautiful
So short-lived

AIDS has stripped me raw
Down to the marrow of my bones
Thousands of soft pink petals
Fallen onto cold concrete

I remember
How a mother wept
At her gay son's funeral

And the father sat
Like a stone
In the wall
Of the old church

Jen Lam

JEN LAM is a Vancouver-born poet infamous for burning up poetry stages with her brand of gasoline-induced spoken word performances. When she's not leaving a trail of destruction from coffee houses to bars, she's either at Simon Fraser University completing a degree in Archaeology or down in her East Vancouver gym working on her kickboxing. She's been a fixture in the Vancouver scene for the past 6 years and has self-published a chapbook, *Serial Cockroach*. Her inner-child is presently lost in the foster care system.

loud impatient love

there are many breeds
of love.
some lead to a sprained
heart.
some to an emotional hangover.
others leave you to tame
a new language of laughter.
only one has delivered
me to a
higher caliber of begging
where
I am soft-bellied corn fields
aching for rainfall
silently resenting the sun.

I am here to serve
the rips
in your back other lovers
have belittled.
with
the afternoon cotton heavy
around my ankles
& gratification
softshoeing on my
eyelids
I surrender my wrists
to the backbeat of your lips
so loud
it breaks the skin of your
smile
thumping
& grinding its
gospel
into the altar
that is my hips.

the birds living inside my
moans
will tell you
the sky is just
a really big cage.

& angels
choke on their
glass tongues
tear their dusty wings
out their backs
fall
sordid & profane
onto the earth
begging to be
mortal.

& we
not quite sure
what to do with
our hands & eyes
hide under
the blanket's
itchy grey.
toes curled like
caterpillars inching towards
magnificence
& allow ourselves
the fever bred rhapsody
of being
caught
by this loud impatient love.

I find a small darkness
underneath the strawberry plants.
echoing the refuge
of your neck's cove

always so ready
to receive
my forehead.

the strawberries
are hard & green
but I pick them anyway
they are bitter
& leave
my tongue stinging.
I devour petals
& stems,
gnaw on the bark
of an apple sapling,
rub beetles &
ladybugs into my
gums
in hope they will
quiet the aftertaste.
suck on my loamy fingers
until they are clean.

I am sick for the rest of the weekend
& you can't understand
the flood of garden
that is escaping from
my stomach.

I try to explain
while
clutching the
toilet's
calm, steady
paunch.

I tell you
it's love.
a loud impatient love
that'll embrace
us until we are deaf.

that it is for us
to be passionately human
for the cockroaches
can't seem to get
the hang of
it.

there is a
gardenforestjungleoasis
that awaits our
voracity.

it is for us
to squeeze every
gritty
greasy millet of
life
into our throats
until our guts bellow
this
loud impatient love.

room 114

her feet
confined to a dungeon of silk bars
at infancy in an attempt to
mold her into art
have languished into
a pair of aborted kittens.
now she's confined to a wheelchair
with an alkaline wool blanket on her
lap to conceal the obsolete.

unearthing stories from her
memory plump wrinkles
of when her husband courted
her   at a time & place where
romance was just a rumour hatched
inside the belly of imagination.

or when I was born & I didn't cry for
the first two weeks.
everyone thought I was mute
she told my mother
not to worry   I was just deciding which voice
to use.

I'm one of the
few in this family yarn that
doesn't have her nose   but I'm sure my children will.

at my last visit   one of the nurses
came up to me complaining that
every time they try to give her a
bath she barks in chinese.
arms flailing like an octopus in heat
once she even tried to
bite a nurse   so could I

explain to my great-grandma that
they were just doing their job.
no   I said & walked away.

you see   years ago when
I shared my gauzed scope
at a friend's grab bag suicide,
the wells inside me humid with fear that one day
I might see it too clearly from the other side,
she told me that
it's our job to wash the dirt
off our own bodies & the day we
forget how to wash that dirt away is the
day we let it bury us.

PoPo

there are two types of chinese grandmothers:
one type
that gets their hair permed
into a helmet of
tight unforgiving curls.
& others that get their
hair chopped
into a severe chin-length bob
bluntly parted to the side
& held in place
with 2 bobby pins
fastened directly
behind each ear.

my maternal grandmother
was of the former but before
she was PoPo
stuffing white rabbit candies &
haw flakes into
my sticky hands
& pockets,
before she was
a mother of 9
saving every penny
so she could
send bottles of peanut oil
& melba toast
to her sister-in-law in China
to ward off the predatory blindness
raping the impotent countryside,
before all that was laid
onto her sandalwood shoulders,
she was a girl with pigtails
eyes combed with laughter.

she was full-cheeked
grace.
the ground beneath her
grateful to
take her steps.

the week after her funeral
we gathered
around the kitchen table
looking through photo albums.
someone remarked
how she looked like a
movie star.
she looked like a
gwai mui
& the rest of us
nodded in agreement
for chinese modesty
prevented us from
ever claiming
anything that beautiful
as one of our own.

from your belly into my belly

the stars are running away from us
their light is not drawing towards but
retreating back into their corners.
from the women in my family
this is what their eyes tell me.
the universe's brilliance is faint
when pressed against their struggled lives.

the stoop of their shoulders
tells me that love is heavy.
love will not have you soaring up into the sky's octaves.
its song is low & lulling like tea leaves
slowly bronzing a pot of water.

love is something you learn.
love is a duty
for the women in my family.
cadenced in silence-dipped kisses
behind stranded doors
sleeping in beds passive.
their hearts like cranberries
hold in their tart passion.

but my heart is of broken gardens
fistfuls of aborted bloom
loud with obvious desires.
I believe that love exists only in the
rooms we find it in.
modesty is a hat a few sizes too small for my head.
my stretchmarks are highways inviting
hitchhikers, missionaries & traveling paper salesmen.
but really   I'm not all that different
from the women in my family for
we all agree that love is done not spoken.

I measured my rise out of childhood not
by pencil marks on the doorway
but against the nurturing curves of my mother.
up along her thigh to hip to waist
to breast to shoulder
to earlobes
we missed meeting eye to eye
in that summer of '87.
now I stand large & awkward
amongst the women in my family.
like winter on her silver stilts
they tread with quiet dignity
skirts down to their ankles
to hide the burden on their knees.

spent the night

with a
more-than-friend
but
not-yet-lover
eating burnt
mac & cheese
listening to music in the key of ruby
doing really bad 3 Stooges imitations
& watching who
knows how many Bruce Lee movies
& I said
I should be going
though I really didn't feel like
going & as he was helping
me
with my coat we started
talking about things I didn't even
know I wanted to talk about
like rodeo clowns
& the migration of camels
& the London subway
& all the wonderful ways to eat
grasshoppers
& the Tokyo Stock Exchange
& the cultural impact of shadow puppets
all before
falling asleep on his couch
dreaming under dali's canvass
until his kisses on my eyelids
corrupt my sleep
he's already dressed for work
there's coffee in the kitchen
he'll be back before six tonight
& if I feel like it maybe we

could go out for sushi
or better yet
there's this new
Jamaican restaurant
just up the street. . . .
as his kiss
on my forehead scatters
I get this feeling of good
this feeling of right
this feeling of going to the supermarket
& getting a cart
whose wheels aren't stuck.

soy sauce baby

then your ex-girlfriend
led by casual cleavage
shows up at your door.
clothes begging to release
her into
your
lap.
a spare face and
toothbrush crude with
anticipation in her
purse.   you leave me
pecking on fried rice.
the kitchen's fluorescent scream
amplified in the empty seat across
from me.   while you walk
her back to her car.   you said,
           it'll just take a minute

one minute
swells into
four
seven
twelve
sixteen.
you return
sit down
sweep rice
into
your mouth
with
blaring
con-cen-tra-tion.

it wouldn't bother me so much.
if only

you weren't tilting your head that
way.   it's as if you
want me to
notice the smudge
of her lipstick on your collar.

I say,
she's pretty.
          you say,
          what's that supposed to mean?
I say
nothing. I'm just saying that she's pretty.
          you say,
          well, she's smart too. and funny.
I say,
yeah, sure. a sense of humour. that's the first thing I noticed.
          you say,
          what's your problem?

and so begins
the random punching of buttons
like a couple of 4 yr. olds let loose
in a hotel elevator.
the skin of our voices
blistering in
this toxic arousal.
it won't be long before
knuckles and palms
find their way
into our slingshot roar.
from the rim of madness
my tongue finds
the clean sense to say,
it's over
and I run home
before I can change my mind.

the tears are too
easy in my eyes
as easy as Harlem
in your bones
greasing your steps
to my door.
I hear you knocking
and talking
  and crying
   and yelling
    and pleading
     and crying
      and cursing
       and crying
        and leaving

            and leaving.

  but I'd rather
  live in a closet of hurricanes
  than believe that
  the blood breaking in my veins
  is love.

  I'd rather
  fall asleep between
  the devil's toes
  than spend my nights
  welding words
  into clumsy handles
  for a casket of a desire.

  I'd rather
  gag on the fumes
  of my rage
  than shrink my life
  in a soak of violence.

so soy sauce baby,
move on to the next table.
this feast of bamboo legs
and lotus lips
doesn't need any of your
seasoning.

Fred Wah

FRED WAH was born in Swift Current, Saskatchewan in 1939, and grew up in the West Kootenay region of British Columbia. He studied at the University of British Columbia in the early 1960s where he was one of the founding editors of the poetry newsletter *TISH*. After graduate work in literature and linguistics at the University of New Mexico in Albuquerque and the State University of New York at Buffalo, he returned to the Kootenays in the late 1960s where he was the founding co-ordinator of the writing program at David Thompson University Centre. He now teaches at the University of Calgary. He has been editorially involved with a number of literary magazines over the years, such as *Open Letter* and *West Coast Line*. He has published seventeen books of poetry. His book of prose-poems, *Waiting For Saskatchewan*, received the Governor General's Award in 1986 and *So Far* was awarded the Stephanson Award for Poetry in 1992. *Diamond Grill*, a biofiction about hybridity and growing up in a small-town Chinese-Canadian café, was published in 1996 and won the Howard O'Hagan Award for Short Fiction.

ArtKnot Thirty Six

Looks like the Angel got through. Wrapped.
Swaddled. In between the rock and the river.

Seen speaking as having been given mere fact.
Mirroring on the wall, *not me*, begrunden.

Watch who'd turned us round, turning and stopping
forever taking leaves from the bottom of the tree.

Spectacle of Mrs. Erickson's totem. Private parts.
Thread round desire like a crack through the cup.

Stare, stare—nothing there. Camp. Earth. House.
Poof! said the beak. Not a ripple. By a hair.

ArtKnot Forty Nine

the steps
for flavour

(a little) sleight of tongue
impossibly meant itself

puente questo
the "you" that shadows every cloud

but it is possible
nothing at all happens

is it not it
the storm the mind

some trill remembered
crests the labial beach

no hay paso

ArtKnot Sixty Nine

what goes up
as they . . .
Hey sailor
wanna
see me
in the third
person let
the rivers run
let the semen
flower far
out in the open
ranging from
here to kingdom
come around
again some
time we could
try that dance
you know the one

Music at the Heart of Thinking One Oh Eight

Now I know I have a heart because it's broken but should I fix it now to
keep it strokin, or should I hear each piece as it is spoken and stoke heart,s
heat so hot I smell it smokin, or could this clock made up of parts be jokin,
that missing spark a mis-read gap provokin, and little sock of baby breath
not chokin, the piggy bank of words much more than tokens not just the
gossip love is always cloaked in nor all the meaning text is usually soaked in
but roast potatoes for a tender button so much depends upon the things
unspoken and if the heart is just this clock around which clusters all that,s
not and if the of and to an in that it is I for be was as can set these el em en t,s
far apart so all the floods are fierce and floral fl,s and hasten slowly stops me
at my selves right now I,ll have an egg because I know its yolks inside and
what I have to do is crack it open.

Music at the Heart of Thinking One Two Seven

No mass is without something else, something added, other. The one and the many. Taste is a gradation of foreignicity: we come across some abandoned specific with the realization that it isn't represented in the sphere of culture surrounding us. These particles of recognition and desire, subalterns and alternatives, solids that could melt into air, are what we use to intervent and domesticate those homogeneous aggregates of institution and industry that surround us.

The shoulders of eating, the sack full of ginger, the Blakean beach, the other word at the end of the word, the curl from kulchur, the grade for the course, the genome in their home, the rap at the door, the spoon full of the rice, the chop for the lick, the tongue in a knot, the circuits of surplus, the milk on the way, the valley and then the valley, the time of the day, the middle of world.

Race, to go

What's yr race
      and she said
what's yr hurry
how 'bout it cock
                           asian man
I'm just going for curry.

You ever been to ethni-city?
How 'bout multi-culti?

          You ever lay out skin
          for the white gaze?

What are you, banana
or egg? Coconut
maybe?

Something wrong Charlie
Chim-chong-say-wong-lung-chung?
You got a slant to yr marginal eyes?

You want a little rice with that garlic?
Is this too hot for you?

          Or slimy or bitter or smelly or tangy or raw or sour

—a little too dirty

          on the edge ~~hiding underneath~~ crawling up yr leg stuck

between the fingernails?

Is that a black hair in yr soup?

Well how you wanna handle this?

You wanna maintain a bit of differ-énce?
Keep our mother's other?
Use the father for the fodder?

What side of John A. MacDonald's tracks you on anyway?

How fast you think this train is going

                           to go?

Words for Prairie

nose for alfalfa
and sage hills
distant
all that
the eye can

daughter
beside me
not looking,
looking

why get it
just right
here?

Whenever I open up for him (so he

can sleep in) early morning's dark eternal neon Wurlitzer shadowing the
empty booths detonates with kicking the kitchen door a starting-pistol crack
all through the café I know I'm both only me and all of me at full stride up
the aisle with clean cotton coffee-filter sacks and an arm-load of saucers
echoed ache of brass plate in my leg eternal, ready Freddy, open up with a
good swift toe to the wooden slab that swings between the Occident and
Orient to break the hush of the whole café before first light the rolling gait
with which I ride this silence that is a hyphen and the hyphen is the door.

On the edge of Centre. Just off Main.

Chinatown. The cafés, yes, but further back, almost hidden, the ubiquitous Chinese store—an unmoving stratus of smoke, dusky and quiet, clock ticking. Dark brown wood paneling, some porcelain planters on the windowsill, maybe some goldfish. Goldfish for Gold Mountain men. Not so far, then, from the red carp of their childhood ponds. Brown skin stringy salt-and-pepper beard polished bent knuckles and at least one super-long fingernail for picking. Alone and on the edge of their world, far from the centre, no women, no family. This kind of edge in race we only half suspect as edge. A gap, really. Hollow.

I wander to it, tagging along with my father or with a cousin, sent there to get a jar of some strange herb or balm from an old man who forces salted candies on us or digs for a piece of licorice dirtied with grains of tobacco from his pocket, the background of old men's voices sure and argumentative within this grotto. Dominoes clacking. This store, part of a geography, mysterious to most, a migrant haven edge of outpost, of gossip, bavardage, foreign tenacity. But always in itself, on the edge of some great fold.

In a room at the back of the Chinese store, or above, like a room fifteen feet over the street din in Vancouver Chinatown, you can hear, amplified through the window, the click-clacking of mah-jong pieces being shuffled over the table tops. The voices from up there or behind the curtain are hot-tempered, powerful, challenging, aggressive, bickering, accusatory, demeaning, bravado, superstitious, bluffing, gossipy, serious, goading, letting off steam, ticked off, fed up, hot under the collar, hungry for company, hungry for language, hungry for luck, edgy.

His half-dream in the still-dark breathing silence is

the translation from the bitter-green cloudiness of the winter melon soup in his dream to the sweet-brown lotus root soup he knows Shu will prepare later this morning for the Chinese staff in the café. He moves the taste of the delicate nut-like lotus seeds through minor degrees of pungency and smokiness to the crunchy slices of lotus root suspended in the salty-sweet beef broth. This silent rehearsal of the memory of taste moves into his mind so that the first language behind his closed eyes is a dreamy play-by-play about making beef and lotus root soup. Simple: a pound of short ribs and a pound of lotus root in a small pot of water with some soy sauce and salt, a little sliced ginger, maybe a few red Chinese dates. Shu will surely touch it with a piece of dried tangerine peel because it's close to Christmas. He feels his tongue start to move as his mouth waters at the palpable flavour of words.

Paul Ching Lee

PAUL CHING LEE
lives in Port Moody,
B.C. He was born
near Guangzhou,
China in 1949, but
has lived in Canada
since he was ten. His
poems and translations
have appeared in *Prism
international*, the *New
Orleans Review,* and
most recently in the
Chinese-Canadian
anthology *Many-
Mouthed Birds*. He is
currently working on
the English translation of
his mother's favourite Sung
Dynasty poets, and para-
fiction on the Cumberland
communities on Vancouver
Island during the late 1800s.

Beach Avenue

The light bows to the hour:
Blue marrow, blue air.

Remnant of cirrus.
A smudge of evening star begins to rise.

To the west, mountains,
Islands in the cool bifold of water.

Almost now, you hear the maples,
Photoelectric,
Leaves in the wholeness of light
Massing night.

Daughters

I fold your hands
into blossoms.

Your fingers unfurl
a northern summer.

Your voice, fern tips, river rocks.

The sea salt lifting
On the eve of my fiftieth year.

Fall

The morning distilling sunlight,
The morning knows
This bloodlight, a quadrant
Of a year begins as rust of bells.

From the trees
Ashes hang silently.
A canopy wind drives
entrails into nostrils, lungs,
The deciduous air stalls.

Equinox, burial of birds,
The tempered leaves,
One blunt eye organizes the fall:
Horizon, broken in the knees.

Night Poem

I, too, dream the husk of dreams
Refugees, the soft rain on my back.
From here the sieved air falls,
Words etched on mouth,
Utterances, bright strands of wind.

As always, I return to this room,
Rummage the hands of the ones sleeping.
The wall rusting lightfall,
The thin bed greets me,
Its dark voice fastened on my skin.

Our only child, her face lifted from shadows,
Slowly unmasking the stones.

North Vancouver

At night the windows are caves
Shuttling fire across this inlet.

Birds re-entering the forest.
Birds carrying stones, amulets of tears
Inlaid with shadows.

The days further into our veins.
Murmur of farewell, ways of moths, the wind
Hovers over our head.

Equinox, we wake to a season upended.
The sun in the doorway,
Mementos on our skin,

A matrix of brave faces,
We leave in time, merely
From a room that no longer knows us,

Not our silences, the way
Our eyes follow the crossfall of rain
As if the whole world is drowning.

October

Tell Wang Wei to meet us,
After the fall
When leaves rise like locusts,
When ashes tighten our skin, we prostrate
Over graves, roots woven into names,
Flagstones, dreams conflate to fog
Buffeted by rain. We sing in sorrow.

Tell his servants
To bring wine and chrysanthemums,
Unfinished poems, too, mired
In fear, the ancestral lamp flickers like stillborn,
The earth trundled in shame, chastened
In the nether world.

Refuge: Cordova Bay

They enter: thin ghosts of men,
Of meteorites
That sang like cicadas in August,
The pine and high road bow to each other,
Their dust woven as one.

Behind your house,
An acre of thistles and swollen plums
Waits to be subdivided. Further west,
A moon scuttles across the cove,
The warped air reappears,
Whirls like a tongue on the rain-stung hills.

The open belly of the coast
Is a woman's eye. It watches
Over empty rooms, aches into the long night
And all the days charged in prayers
While birds gather blades of sadness
Grown like the jaded weeds of Y'in.

Below the cliff,
The ashes have collected the years,
Stalked the whereabouts of a name:
        It is nowhere.
Now the wind lengthens on foreheads,
Night moves the exiled blood a breath nearer
To bright water, spillway of horizons.

Jim Wong-Chu

JIM WONG-CHU was born in Hong Kong in 1949, first sighted on Canadian soil at the age of three, and spent his childhood and adolescence in various Chinese cafés throughout North America. His nomadic existence ended with his return to Vancouver in the late 1960s where he experience a mind-altering identity crisis and has been on a spiritual quest ever since. He has wandered the eighteen levels of Chinatown hell in the guise of community activist, historian, radio broadcaster ("Pender Guy"), literary jurist, poet (*Inspection of a House Paid in Full* and *Chinatown Ghosts*), and co-editor of anthologies (*Many-Mouthed Birds* and *Swallowing Clouds*). His latest incarnation finds him as a founding member and president of the Asian Canadian Writers' Workshop, an organization dedicated to helping young writers to publish their work.

how feel I do?

your eyes plead approval
on each utter word

and even my warmest smile
cannot dispel the shamed muscles
from your face

let me be honest
with you

to tell the truth
I fell very much at home
in your embarrassment

don't be afraid

like you
I too was mired in another language
and I gladly surrender it
for english

you too
in time
will lose your mother's tongue

and speak
at least as fluent
as me
now tell me

how do you feel?

ice

was the first time
anyone remembers it happening

the fields froze
in our village
in south china

we broke some
not knowing what it was
and took it to the junk peddler

he thought it was glass
and traded us a penny
for it

he wrapped it up
in old cloth and placed it
on top of his basket

of course
the noon day sun melted it

by the time
we came back with more
he had gotten wise

mother

she always wears her silence
in front of father

funny tho

none of us
brothers or sisters
ever woke
when they made love
and that must have been often
because there are many of us
and some knew they were not wanted

those were the days
before birth control pills
and condoms
at least the cheap ones

we were poor

funny tho

father never gave her money
to buy food
preferring to buy it himself
but she fed us
I never understood this

in the morning
she'd be up before us
fixing our breakfast *jook*
and after packing us off to school
she'd start her wash
by hand
cold soap water

wooden wash board
hand wrung
headless forms hung on bamboo poles
skewered shirtsleeves like flags
rows of crucifixes
baking in the dry wind

the day is long
with many goodbyes and hellos
before the night

while we sleep
in our one room home

she mends the last of tomorrow's shirts
and quietly waits

for father

the newspaper vending kwan yin

1
she got her bedroom eyes
from
selling papers

in front of yen fong's
at
eight below

her bloodless face
unpainted
cracks
at the break of dawn

2
your every turn brings you closer
to her

busy street

the surge forces the air
into
a thinning corridor

her hand outstretched
before you

3
you tempt her
with
a large bill

(she loves forgotten money)

so
naturally
she short-changes you

(surtax on the careless)

4
you catch her
but
before you can act

she swallows your tongue

your mind raging
in the wind

5
in a world
of
unrepentant sinners

buddhas
must survive

there is no malice in this game
she is not
your lover
and
owes you nothing

you will understand

when you see her
at
the end of day

dragging her shadow
softly
through the rain

---

kwan yin: goddess of mercy

equal opportunity

in early canada
when railways were highways

each stop brought new opportunities

there was a rule

>   the chinese could only ride
>   the last two cars
>   of the trains

that is

until a train derailed
killing all those
in front

(the chinese erected an altar and thanked buddha)

a new rule was made

>   the chinese must ride
>   the front two cars
>   of the trains

that is

until another accident
claimed everyone
in the back

(the chinese erected an altar and thanked buddha)

after much debate
common sense prevailed

the chinese are now allowed
to sit anywhere
on any train

recipe for tea

pronounce: téh or tèá
origin: fukienese/scottish dialects

a modest pot
enough for
four
small cups

insert tea

green or fermented
or in a
bag

        (the first ships came to trade)

        the area was fukien
        the traders were scottish

the water
boiled separately

        brought it back
        bastardized it
        made it mud
        drowned in heavy cream
        two, three teaspoons
        of colonial sugar

keep your eyes
on the bubbles

shrimp eyes
crab eyes
fish eyes

in search for monopoly
planted in india
after their first crop:

                                opium

the optimum is
crab eyes

crab
clattering
before
fish
winking

            (the second ships brought my forefathers)

            high tea
            high civilized tea
            biscuits
            crumpets
            crystallized ginger
            fragrant cinnamon spices

note:

the first pour
is not for drink

            the best known tea party
            was in boston

            the tea was chinese
            but none invited

pour only
to
cleanse
and awaken

steep briefly

discard

                    (the third ships brought me)

the second pour: discovery

the third pour: exhilaration

the final pour: afterthought

if

desired

repeat

ACKNOWLEDGEMENTS

Andy Quan would like to thank all of the poets of *Swallowing Clouds* whose words impress and inspire me; everyone who assisted at Arsenal Pulp Press, especially Brian for his vision and patience; Geremie, John Michael, and other friends who helped me with *my* words in this anthology; and the venerable Jim Wong-Chu for inviting me to hop aboard this project. A special acknowledgement to the amazing Quan family: Joe, Hilda, Walter, Tom, and Kimiko.

PUBLICATION CREDITS

Louise Bak: All poems are from her book *Gingko Kitchen* (Toronto: Coach House Books, 1997), reprinted with permission of the author.

Lien Chao: All poems appear in *Maples and the Stream: A Bilingual Long Narrative Poem* (Toronto: TSAR Publications, 1999), reprinted with permission of the author.

Ritz Chow: "a fall of grief," "something chinese," "upon receipt of j's letter," and "repetitions for a younger woman" were first published in *Contemporary Verse 2*. "Incantation" was first published in *Pearls of Passion: A Treasury of Lesbian Erotica*, edited by C. Allyson Lee and Makeda Silvera (Toronto: Sister Vision, 1994).

Fiona Tinwei Lam: "Camouflage" was first published in *A Room at the Heart of Things*, edited by Elizabeth Harvor (Montreal: Véhicule, 1998). "Mourning" and "An Ordinary Place" were first published in *The Literary Review of Canada*.

Evelyn Lau: All poems are from her book *Oedipal Dreams* (Victoria: Beach Holme Publishers, 1992; reissue: Toronto: Gutter, 1999), reprinted with permission of Gutter Press.

Leung Ping-Kwan: "An Old Colonial Building," "The Leaf on the Edge," and "Seagulls of Kunming" are from his book *City at the End of Time* (1992). "Soup with Dried Cabbage," "Eggplants," and "Sushi for Two" are from his book *Foodscape* (1997). "Monster City" and "China Doll" are from his book *Clothink* (1998). Reprinted with permission of the author.

Thuong Vuong-Riddick: All poems are from her book *Two Shores/Deux Rives* (Vancouver: Ronsdale, 1995), reprinted with permission of Ronsdale Press.

Fred Wah: "Whenever I open up for him (so he," "On the edge of Centre. Just off Main," and "His half-dream in the still-dark breathing silence is" are from his book *Diamond Grill* (Edmonton: NeWest, 1996), reprinted with permission of the author.

Rita Wong: All poems except "chaos feary" are from her book *monkeypuzzle* (Vancouver: Press Gang Publishers, 1998), reprinted with permission of Press Gang Publishers.

Jim Wong-Chu: All poems except "recipe for tea" are from his book *Chinatown Ghosts* (Vancouver: Arsenal Pulp, 1986).

Paul Yee: "Kamloops Chinese Cemetery (July 1977)," "Hastings Express, 10 pm" "Operation," and "Spences Bridge, B.C." were first pubished in *West Coast Review*. "Last Words II" and "The Grass Dragon" were first published in *Inalienable Rice: A Chinese & Japanese Canadian Anthology* (Vancouver: Powell Street Revue and the Chinese Canadian Writers Workshop, 1979).

PHOTO CREDITS

Marisa Anlin Alps by Lionel Trudel
Ritz Chow by Jacquelyne Luce
Lydia Kwa by Louié Ettling
Larissa Lai by Monika Kin Gagnon
Laiwan by Lynne Wanyeki
Jen Lam by Jim Wong-Chu
Evelyn Lau by Lorne Bridgman
Pei Hsien Lim courtesy B.C. Persons With AIDS Society
Andy Quan by Keith Shaw